In nature, there exists two fundamental forces that sustain all living beings on Earth: yin chi and yang chi. In our ancient past, masters have discovered how to harness these hidden forces, utilizing them to bend the perceived boundaries of ordinary life.

Readers are urged instead to learn from Mo Pai, and to observe the underlying mechanics of this technology. Ultimately, conscious immortality is the goal, but one should not be limited in their resources. Going forward is a step-by-step analysis of the ancient esoteric art known as Mo Pai.

ENTER

MO PAI

The Ancient Training of the Immortals

James Van Gelder

Cover design provided by Nat Monney

Website: http://NatMonney.DeviantArt.com/

CONTENTS

Foreword

Achieving what one might call a *historical* level of greatness requires nothing short of an awakening. Men like John Chang and Jim McMillan stand as beacons in this regard; the legacy of their years of discipline is like an immortal fruit fastidiously nurtured to perfection, and they have both become modern legends for having sown such seeds. These men are in sync with something intangibly real at the heart of the human condition, and the path that they share is so elemental that neither time nor distance can dilute its potency. Their teachings offer glimpses of transcendence, and their achievements allow all of us to have a palpable taste of hope.

In this same vein, we find ourselves in front of another teacher; a man who's studied the lessons of Chang and McMillan, along with countless others, and now works to guide and elevate us all. *Enter Mo Pai* weaves a seasoned spiritual practitioner's understanding of energy with the knowledge found in the ancient teachings of chi cultivation, allowing Van Gelder to offer us one of the most valuable perspectives on Mo Pai put forth thus far—making these lessons indispensable. With *Enter Mo Pai*, Van Gelder's practiced eye seems to have created something that is beyond honest, something that effortlessly teems with life saving tips:

something that simply cannot hide its importance.

I never would have guessed how deeply *Enter Mo Pai* could manage to resonate with me. When Van Gelder first contacted me for permission to quote *Seeking the Master of Mo Pai*, I agreed but couldn't help burying this willingness under a mountain of caution and fatherly advice—so hard is it to shake the respect I've developed for these teachings. So, at first, I sought to guide and share my aid with a fellow teacher. But I soon noticed, as I began digging into the work in search for ways to help, that its voice was remarkably clear, and that its multitude of lessons were coming to me as indispensable allies—particularly, its message regarding patience. I realized that the caution I'd first felt was a sensation that I not only shared with Van Gelder, but it's one that he'd already expertly crafted into his work so that any readers might be properly braced for the potent knowledge waiting within the Mo Pai system.

As well, I found Van Gelder's work to be teaming with practical wisdom—something which seems to be in short supply in today's world of chi development. The inward journey is one of healing, as it is a path that is profound and individualized, and we find that these aspects are artfully addressed in *Enter Mo Pai*. The work also takes the time to shine a light on some of Mo Pai's more troublesome areas: the misleading ideas and dangerous misapplications of the practice—which is one of the reasons I feel Van Gelder's work is so relevant. He has an ideal perspective to help navigate what's become a contextual gray area, a place that eludes appropriate definition for many who are attracted to the internal arts, and he does so with a palette that is rich with bright insights and bold assessments. With *Enter Mo Pai,* we've been given a work that not only shows us a way to find the beauty of Mo Pai, but one that teaches us how to avoid the ugliness and the derelict misapplications that only hurt their practitioners.

Personally, my martial arts training began at an early age. Over the years, I refined my skills in the arts of Tai Chi and Ba Gua all the way up until I met Mo Pai practitioner Jim McMillan in 2011. McMillan was a man committed to helping his students develop to their fullest potential, which was a trait that I graciously benefited from. Since that period, I've published a number of books on chi development, including McMillan's own *Seeking the Master of Mo Pai: Adventures with John Chang.* My path has shown me that having a great teacher or source of information can be such a tremendous boon for the striving individual, and this is why these teachers and their works have the remarkable value they do; a value that is particularly high in this troubled modern-day world.

There is an energy disease affecting our planet; signposts can be found in any one of humanity's countless daily desertions from righteousness, and where they all point is to a world ecology that's quickly slipping away into ruins. These signs are endemic to humans simply because we have fallen from grace. We all see the immense suffering, and it's compromising the suspended bridge of our delicate experiences. However, the climate is shifting. Many are approaching reality in terms of energy and consciousness, and Mo Pai is at the helm of this global tide of transformation. The demonstrations by John Chang exist as some of the most widespread and scientifically indisputable evidence of chi manipulation in history, and every one he gives helps to grow the global consciousness and move us away from an ecological collapse.

Today, Mo Pai is seeing a surge in interest thanks to the work of Chang, McMillan, and now Van Gelder. However, it's no stretch to say that a great teacher is still hard to find. I've encountered this problem myself in instructors who lack either noteworthy technique or adequate language to convey their mastery. One can't help but find sadness when imagining that with the countless students out there seeking masters of their own, those few who *have* mastered the internal arts can so rarely pass their prowess along.

Wilhelm Reich said in his book *Listen, Little Man!*, "You differ from a great man in only one respect: the great man was once a very little man, but he developed one important quality: he recognized the smallness and narrowness of his thoughts and actions." Truly, we all have the capacity for greatness. There have been patriarchs, saints, prophets, and healers who have forever enhanced life for humans on Earth, yet the important thing to remember is that there will be more. We all have the capacity to wind down the list of excuses and build up the courage to fully embody pure and golden white-light. It's so encouraging to see that the greatness we are seeking, that which can save our very lives and afterlives, can be found here. *Enter Mo Pai* offers a stabilizing hand to help practitioners develop towards collective upliftment. I hope you will enjoy reading it as much as I did.

-Derrick Arnold, 2015

Introduction

EIGHT-WAYS THUNDER BOXING, also known as Mo Pai, is an ancient system of internal cultivation that began over two thousand years ago with a man named Mo Tzu.[1] Since its incarnation, this system has been continually refined by successions of ancient sages until the precise method was perfected for successfully combining the yin and yang chi inside of man. Once combined, the yin and yang chi create a form of "electric chi" capable of being utilized for a myriad of different applications including healing, combat, and even transcending the cycle of death and rebirth. It is understood that once fusion of the two energies (yin chi and yang chi) has been successfully attained, the individual is then able to retain their human characteristics[2] after the death of the physical body.

There are four main stages of development to the process of creating the immortal fusion inside of the practitioner's being.[3] These initial stages have been taught to westerners as level one, two, three, and four. The final stage, level four, is the stage of the immortal fusion. However, beyond level four, there are seventy-two levels to the Mo Pai system in total. So, when put into proper perspective, the great immortal fusion that is the signature of Mo Pai is actually only the beginning: a door that opens one into a new world.

Currently, the greatest Mo Pai practitioner that is physically alive today is Master John Chang. Master Chang was last estimated to be at level twenty-two of the seventy-two levels. Having achieved fusion, John Chang has transcended death and is able to harness and control the powerful "electric chi."

Akin to a traditional Native American medicine man, John Chang typically utilizes his supernatural abilities in order to conduct healing treatments at no monetary cost to his patients. However, John Chang will typically utilize his electric qi in conjunction with acupuncture. By channeling his electric qi through acupuncture needles that are positioned at specific points on the body, Chang is able to dramatically stimulate his patient's meridian healing system. This process amplifies the body's regenerative potential and results in seemingly impossible feats of healing. It is a dichotomy of the modern world that perhaps the single most potent form of medicine today is both ancient in nature and is being performed free of charge.

In an effort to teach his students, John Chang also uses his powers in order to demonstrate the destructive power of his art. This sometimes involves him focusing his chi at objects and causing them to burst into flames. These supernatural feats have been famously displayed on many YouTube videos as well as the 1988 documentary *The Ring of Fire: An Indonesian Odyssey*.

Following the release of the video footage of John

Chang's abilities, two primary western students, Jim McMillan and Kosta Danaos, travelled to visit him directly and learn the training firsthand. These two primary students both had long periods of direct contact with a true living master of the Mo Pai tradition, and during their training they recorded invaluable information and experiences regarding both energy cultivation and meditation training.

The written accounts of their experiences studying under John Chang are found in *Seeking the Master of Mo Pai: Adventures with John Chang* by Jim McMillan, and *The Magus of Java: Teachings of an Authentic Taoist Immortal* by Kosta Danaos. The information documented in these two works serve as an important foundation when approaching an understanding of Mo Pai. Ultimately, however, these books are just a piece of the puzzle; to be a true seeker one has to compile information from all sources available.

Cultivation

For the dedicated practitioner Mo Pai serves as both a fighting art and as a catalyst for metamorphosis, constantly evolving the practitioner both externally and internally. The accumulation of life-force involved with the Mo Pai practices does not only cause one to become more powerful, but it also enhances and clarifies the practitioner on an experiential level. Eventually, with enough persistent training, meditation leads one to the steps of immortality with a realization of one's true nature and the experience of nirvana.

Introduction

What is the goal of meditation?

"Get to the stage to know the primal self."

–Kosta Danaos[4]

Through consistent training, John Chang has been able to consciously ascend himself into the ranks of the immortals. As such, besides the fantastic powers, John Chang has unlocked his primal self, and he now serves as a beacon of light for humans.

> "I know if I lived near him I would probably want to be around him as much as I could as well, he is really a strange and wonderful man, one that you instinctively want to be around."

> –Jim McMillan[5]

Knowing the primal self is not an idea, but an actual experience. It is an attainment that is regarded as the purpose of one's very existence. An experience at the depth of one's true immortal nature, the "primordial self." However, most do not have a substantial reference point when making an effort to understand the importance of self-cultivation and following truth. It is for this reason that most people do not take the wisdom of ancient masters seriously and fail to commit themselves to continual practice. If one is able to reach self-realization, either through traditional practices or through the Mo Pai training, the practitioner will not simply "know" who they are, but actually will *become* who they are. A complete experiential transformation. An immortal being such as this is now a spirit with a human body. A being who has died[6] but continues to live.

The Etheric Body

To most westerners, the etheric body is an unknown aspect of ourselves, but contains within it the capacity to unlock seemingly unlimited amounts of power. To understand the etheric body is to understand the mechanics of Mo Pai's great power, the secret of which lies in its activation.

> "When I was studying Nei Kung at that time we didn't know there was an enteric nervous system, which would explain what we were feeling. Basically, what you're doing is your programming a separate self. All of a sudden you have a nervous structure that can accept this, it is actually more powerful than our spine."
>
> –Kosta Danaos[7]

In all individuals, the etheric body continually works for one's highest good, constantly gathering and refining the vital energy contained in their surroundings. During Mo Pai training, the practitioner takes advantage of this process by utilizing certain techniques that allow them to consciously absorb large amounts of chi into their etheric body from the surrounding environment.

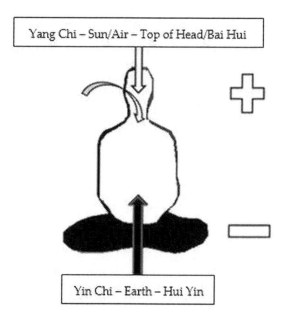

Both yin chi and yang chi flow within the etheric body. The vital energy known as yang chi, continually enters through the back section of the top of the head. This point of entry is known as **Bai Hui.** One method that practitioners use to find this point is by touching the top of one's ears with their thumbs and then touching the middle fingers together at the top of the head where it feels energetically active.

After entering the top of the head, the yang chi descends down the individual's back and into the lower dantien, which serves as a container for holding and distributing the vital energy to the body. This constant inflow of yang chi is the reason that the back section of the top of the head is always warm. In meditation, when the awareness has extended into the etheric body, it actually becomes possible to perceive the inflowing waves of warm chi as it travels down the back. The Bai Hui point is also a natural balancing mechanism for the body to convert excess yin chi into yang chi.

Yang chi needs to be equally balanced with yin chi. Yin chi is absorbed from the earth by the body at the **Hui Yin point**. The Hui Yin point is located near the area of the perineum.[8] Similar to the Bai Hui point, the Hui Yin point is also where the body transforms yin chi into yang chi. For this reason the Hui Yin point and the Bai Hui point are means for the body to balance the yin and yang chi in order to maintain harmony.

Humans also gather vital energy through the air that they breathe and the food that they eat. Many monks will eat with constant awareness, knowing food contains a concentration of vital energy that is absorbed when consumed. Some alchemists state that it is important to give intent and to "charge" the food that one consumes, so as to transmute the vital energy contained in the food in order to fit one's desires.[9]

Structure

The basic structure of the etheric body contains three dantiens as well as seven major chakras. The Chakra system and Dantien system are inter-connected and develop naturally in an ascending fashion from the bottom of the spine upwards to the top of the head. In cultivation, one must lay his/her foundation in order to reach the heavens.

There are three main localities, or containers, for the vital energy that is absorbed from one's environment. While residing on a subtle frequency, the three dantiens are similar to organs and are made of tissue. Depending on how refined the vital energy has become, it will reside in either the lower dantien, middle dantien, or upper dantien.

The structure of one's development in energy cultivation is similar to the pyramid depicted on the back of the United States dollar bill. The lowest part of the pyramid is the foundation and is known as the lower dantien,[10] This dantien holds the largest amount of vital energy. The middle section of the pyramid, or the middle dantien, holds less energy. Finally, the highest section of the pyramid, the upper dantien, holds the least energy; though it is also the brightest and has a shining affect.

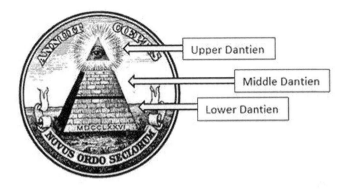

If one looks closely at the dollar, there is also an eye on the pyramid. This is significant because when the three dantiens and seven chakras have been cultivated, the mystical "third eye" becomes awakened on the forehead of the practitioner. This eye does not reside on the physical frequency and is not ordinarily visible, however, at this stage, the third eye is so distinct to the practitioner that it feels as if it were a physical eye.

Many cultivation practices, including Mo Pai, simply refer to the vital energy that flows through the chakra system and the danten system as Chi. While it is not necessary with regards to the Mo Pai training to differentiate the different aspects of the vital energy known as Chi, it can actually help one to gain an understanding towards energy cultivation in general that they can then relate with life. Just understand that when the book moves into the actual training everything will once again be universally referred to as chi so as to stay consistent with the original Mo Pai teachings.

Taoist alchemy further breaks down the different

subtleties of the vital substance, commonly referred to as chi, into what is known as the "three elixirs." The three dantiens contain, accumulate, as well as refine the three "elixirs." The three elixirs are known as jing, chi, and shen in Taoist alchemy.

The lower dantien houses the most unrefined form of energy which is termed jing or "ching" by Taoist alchemists. Jing is responsible for the vitality of the physical body and is reflected by the health of a person's teeth. Jing is both thick and hot in feeling because it is the most unrefined form of vital energy. In Taoist cultivation terms, it is *jing* which is contained in the lower dantien and is the main concern of the Mo Pai training.[11]

Over time, the jing in the lower dantien is refined into chi: a subtle energy with a temperature that is more difficult to discern that resides in the middle dantien. Chi is responsible for a person's dynamism and is reflected by the glow of the skin.

The last elixir is known as shen. Shen is responsible for inner awareness, or spirit, and is reflected by the glowing of the eyes.[13] A person at this high degree of cultivation also has a halo that is visible on a subtle level, similar to the light around the top of the pyramid.

Each of the three dantiens serve as a locality for the continual refinement and storage of each frequency of vital energy. Continually transforming jing to chi, and finally chi to shen. When the three containers, or dantiens, are full, one begins to cultivate ling, which is considered ultimate.[13]

At birth, every child begins with a degree of substance in each of the three elixirs, but as time goes on, many lose sight of their inner vision and begin to develop backwards. Only a very select few retain shen from a young age as they grow older. Many begin losing shen (upper dantien) to supply chi (middle dantien), and then finally losing chi to supply jing (lower dantien). This is aging, both physically and consciously, but humans do not have to age this way if they can reverse the process and restore the three elixirs.

By activating the seven chakras and restoring the three elixirs, the individual activates the fountain of youth. A recycling of the vital energy occurs, keeping the body youthful. A friend of mine would say, "Some people age like a fine wine, while others age like a barrel of gasoline." However, it is important to note that meditation and energy cultivation is not the only path for awakening the etheric system. Mediation and energy cultivation are just direct means to do so.

The seven major Chakras also play a significant role in energy cultivation, constantly working in correlation with the three dantiens. The chakras are similar to whirl pools created by an exchange between the flows of the two opposite energies of yin chi and the yang chi. The rotation of the major chakras move and refine the elixir in each of the three dantiens, creating an energy-field effect that surrounds the student.

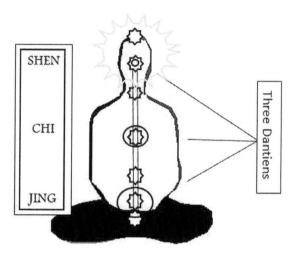

✿ 7 Major Energy Centers

The capacity of the "three elixirs" and the activity of the seven major chakras determine the overall health and youthfulness of the physical body. When the etheric body is at a high potential, the human body will not only last longer, but will have the capability to rejuvenate from disease.

Currently, a basic understanding of the etheric body and its importance on health is a major hole in the western medical paradigm; in the future, learning to activate the etheric body to its higher potential will be a major breakthrough in western medicine.

Scientific progress into our true nature will keep continually moving forward. Today, more and more evolved humans like John Chang are appearing and causing disruptions to the central scientific paradigm. The real importance is that over time by practicing meditation, Mo Pai training, or connecting with one's soul through soul-purpose, people can begin to "program" and awaken their etheric nervous system to higher potentials. This process leads to an increase in the quality of life both physically and on an experiential level.

The Precarious Nature of Mo Pai

Before moving on to the level one training, it is necessary to emphasize the precarious nature of Mo Pai. The art of Mo Pai is without doubt one of the single most fascinating technologies in the energy cultivation arena, but it is not without risk. For the serious practitioner, treading carefully is a must. It is important to understand that Mo Pai is not natural, it is a man-made technology. If trained without proper guidance it can have harmful effects towards one's body. In most cases, simply stopping the training will allow the body to reverse any negative effects.

"The Knowledge of how to train is best kept in secrecy because while many people think they can handle the training, it can actually be very dangerous if done improperly. And this has played out with certain Westerners…"

--Jim McMillan[14]

The main reason that Mo Pai training is potentially dangerous is because throughout the training the practitioner is developing their lower dantien beyond its normal capacity. In the later levels of the training, the lower dantien can be compared to a large water balloon waiting to be popped. If the rules are not followed carefully, then the dantien has the possibility of rupturing. This injury can be serious and not everyone heals appropriately, so those that have trouble healing past disease will have a difficult time moving forward.

In its original form, the system of Mo Pai was taught on a personal basis from teacher to student. In order to be qualified as a teacher, the practitioner had to have progressed past level 4 and attained fusion. Those that attain fusion are able to feel and sense chi, thus allowing them to continually check on their student's progress. This is important so that the student progresses smoothly and avoids any problems. John Chang, the current highest level practitioner of Mo Pai, can even check on his students from across the world. Without this direct guidance from a Mo Pai immortal, serious training would almost involve the practitioner turning his/her own body into a laboratory of which unexpected outcomes cannot be handled by western physicians. However, studying Mo Pai and learning the teachings that John Chang had to share, can open new doors of possibility.

Level One

SUMMONING THE FIRE

Level one of the Mo Pai training consists of specialized meditation in order to accumulate both yang chi and yin chi. The goal at the end of level one is for the lower dantien to be one-hundred percent full of yang chi.

The Mo Pai meditation training is a combination of three primary aspects: concentration, lower abdominal breathing, and grounding.

Moving forward is an analysis of the level one technique that has been released widely through many of the direct western students of John Chang. From those students, Jim McMillan and Kosta Danaos have been the major players when it comes to teaching. Using the information that has been made available by John Chang's students, the level one training can be both observed and analyzed.

Meditation Posture

Sit down with legs crossed in either the full-lotus, half-lotus, or normal cross-legged style. Full-lotus is similar to normal seated position except the practitioner sits with both legs folded so that the back of each foot is resting on top of the opposite thigh. A proper full-lotus position will naturally straighten and align the curvature of the back. Half-lotus is when only one foot rests on top of the opposite thigh, while the other foot rests under the opposite thigh. If the practitioner cannot sit in half lotus, they can also sit with their legs crossed normally and still make significant progress. If one is not in full-lotus posture, they also need to add a hand mudra. The hand mudra serves to increase the potency of the training by raising the awareness.

For many westerners accustomed to the modern lifestyle, the ability to engage in the proper half-lotus or full-lotus posture is limited. These students should not strain themselves or put excess pressure on their knees. One should never force a posture. It is important not to strain the knees and to be patient in developing flexibility. The ability to meditate in lotus/half-lotus comes naturally as a person progresses in conscious awareness. Flexibility runs hand in hand with personal evolution. The further one's training develops, the easier and more natural it becomes to sustain the different asanas.

The idea behind yoga is to stretch in order to evolve consciously. But vice-versa, with conscious evolution comes flexibility. This is because one's mind is the source of dis-ease and tension. As the student becomes more aware and present through continual training, their body also becomes more relaxed. As the muscles become more relaxed they also become more pliable. The point being, students should allow themselves to fall into the postures naturally over time as they progress.

Each of the three sitting postures have different effects on the focus of awareness inside of the etheric body. Normal cross-legged sitting naturally places awareness at the stomach area, also known as Earth. Half-lotus posture places awareness on the heart area, also known as humanity. The final posture, the full-lotus, concentrates the awareness at the top of the head, also known as heaven.[1] [2] This raised awareness fosters a more efficient meditation practice and releases the requirement for a hand mudra. The higher that the awareness is raised, the more control that an individual has in meditation.

By supplementing a hand mudra, the resting awareness of the sitting postures can also be raised, thus increasing the effectiveness of the meditation practice. The most important aspect of the various hand mudras is the thumb itself. The majority of the thumb correlates with the spine, or the column of awareness, and the tip of the thumb corresponds with the top of the head. By utilizing a hand mudra that touches the tip of the thumbs, one is placing awareness at the top of the head and increasing the effectiveness of one's practice. By placing awareness at the top of the head, one is, to a certain extent, fulfilling the purpose of the full-lotus posture.

There are three primary variations of hand mudras which one can employ based on comfort. The first two being very common and the last being somewhat rare.

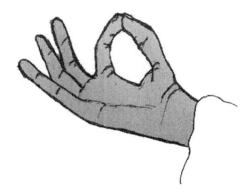

The first hand mudra is connecting the tip of the thumb with the tip of the pointer finger and resting the hands with the palms facing upward.

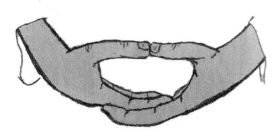

The second mudra is often used in Zen meditation. This mudra is placing the right hand over the left hand with both palms facing up and connecting the tips of the thumbs.

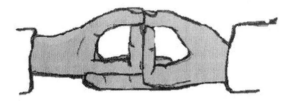

Dhyana Mudra, the last hand mudra, is a combination of the first two. The practitioner places the right hand over the left hand and connects the two thumbs, then raises the two pointer fingers to connect with the tips of the thumbs.

Meditation Preparation

Place hands on the legs or lap, with both hands positioned in the mudra chosen. The spine is kept straight like a column of coins and the shoulders are stretched out like the wings of a vulture in order to keep from hunching forward. The chin should be very slightly pressed in towards the larynx, so as to allow vital-energy to flow into the head.[3]

Meditation Technique

The level one meditation technique first involves becoming aware of the lower dantien. Traditionally, the location of the lower dantien is three finger widths below the naval and two finger widths behind the naval.

The lower dantien is cultivated in the level one meditation training through isolating the breath into the lower stomach so that no other part of the body is moving. If done correctly, one will notice that their shoulders are still, and unmoving. Only the stomach area should be moving with each in-breath and out-breath. Over time, this style of breathing will become second-nature to the practitioner.

The purpose behind the level one breathing technique is because yang chi is in the air that one breaths, so by isolating the breathing into one area (the lower dantien), the practitioner is specifically targeting the purpose of filling the lower dantien.

Note: The Mo Pai student also has the option to practice the "reverse breathing" technique, which is where the stomach actually expands while breathing out and contracts while breathing in. The reverse breathing technique is common in many Daoist cultivation circles for cultivating the LDT (lower dantien).

The next aspect of the level one technique is that during the exercise, the practitioner is visualizing their breath moving in through their nostrils and down into the lower dantien and then back up and out. If the practitioner does not like visualization, however, it is not required and the dantien will still be cultivated as long as the other mechanics are observed. In hermetics, the idea behind visualization practice is that it creates a type of filter altering the structure of the energy being absorbed, thus making it more focused.[4]

During the meditation training, once the two basic mechanics of visualization and breathing are understood, the practitioner is to sustain his/her awareness without "blacking-out" in thought. I refer to one getting lost in thought as "blacking-out," because the practitioner will actually lose their conscious situational awareness of where they are and what they are currently doing and be taken somewhere else by their thoughts. The goal is to have an awareness that is unmoving by the tides of the mind.

The practitioner has the freedom to choose from three primary methods to assist them in sustaining their awareness. The practitioner can choose to either focus on the breath moving in and out, the lower dantien area, or simply rest in awareness and not become attached to thoughts. For many, mastery of the mind can take years of consistent practice, so one should be patient with themselves as the awareness needs time to develop.

Note: Taking into account both the visualization and the isolated breathing, the Mo Pai method is very similar to the breathing techniques used by the ancient Egyptians for similar purposes.[5] The major difference is that the Egyptians would focus their training on all three sections of the lungs. When they focused on the lower dantien area, however, they would isolate their breath by moving only the stomach in the same fashion as the Mo Pai do. Also similar, the Egyptians would utilize visualization training by imagining red breath moving into the lower dantien.[6]

Grounding

Grounding is an important aspect of the Mo Pai training. Level one Mo Pai deals with gathering both yin chi and yang chi. Earth chi, or yin chi, can only be obtained by having direct contact with the earth. As such, the grounding aspect of the Mo Pai training involves being in direct contact with the earth while practicing the meditation technique. The importance of grounding is so that while the practitioner is absorbing yang chi during their training, they are, at the same time, also absorbing yin chi. Yin chi comes from the earth and enters the body through the energy point in the area of the perineum (aka Hui Yin). However, it is an important aspect of Mo Pai to understand that yin chi is not able to pass through insulated material. The practitioner must be making direct contact with the earth. If the student cannot sit directly on the ground, they can sit on a metal plate instead. Simply attach a grounding wire to the metal plate. The metal grounding wire should be connected to either a stake in the ground or a pipe in one's house that is connected to the earth. John Chang mentions that the pipes in most bathrooms will suffice.[7] A common method is to attach a wire (18 gauge or larger, preferably stranded wire) to the cold-water pipe under the sink. Then attach this wire to a sheet of metal and sit in meditation on the metal sheet.

Besides meditation practice, it is important to be grounded while sleeping, and as such, many will duct tape a large sheet of wire mesh to their mattress under their sheets. By connecting the grounding wire to the wire mesh, the individual will be grounded and absorb yin chi while sleeping. Uncoated wire mesh can be purchased at any home improvement store for very cheap.

There are many guides about the grounding process, which also goes by the term "Earthing." In the west, instead of absorbing yin chi, they refer to the phenomenon as absorbing electrons. Either way, being grounded is important for overall health and reducing inflammation in the body. After all, our bodies are large electrical circuits that need to be grounded.

The level one training is designed to assist the practitioner in absorbing both yin chi and yang chi. If not connected to the earth directly, or through a conductive material, Yin chi will become blocked and not be absorbed properly.

When interviewed, Kosta Danaos explains how if a practitioner enters into meditation while sitting on a grounded surface, a wet spot will actually develop on the ground underneath the meditator. This wet spot is from our etheric body absorbing yin chi from the ground.[8] This occurrence is similar to how yang chi causes warmth on the top of the head. The yin chi being absorbed is creating a wet spot to occur on the physical ground. The cultivation of these subtle energies have real and profound effects on our physical reality. Do not expect to achieve water marks right away when practicing meditation. The example provided by Danaos simply provides powerful insight into the power of being connected with the earth.

Lastly, while one should make every effort possible to achieve proper grounding, it is not worthless to train on an insulated surface. In order to progress at a reasonable rate, it is preferable to train *whenever there is opportunity*, instead choosing not to train because of unfavorable conditions. Someone worrying about this aspect will not progress very quickly in any internal art and will often miss opportune chances to progress. For example, waiting on a long bus ride can be transformed into a beneficial training opportunity.

Training

The purpose of level one is to fill up the lower dantien with yang chi. The level one practice achieves this through a mixture of awareness meditation, lower abdomen breathing (or reverse breathing), and proper grounding. Accomplishing level one requires eighty-one hours of absolute meditation. It is estimated that a student who is just beginning can only hold his concentration for 2.2% of the time, which at this rate would take the average practitioner ten years of training at one hour per day.[9]

However, throughout one's training the rate of progress does not remain constant. With continual practice, the effectiveness of the meditation technique actually accelerates over time. This is because the practitioner's awareness is increasing with practice. They stop becoming lost in thought as often, and remain stable in awareness for longer periods of time. As the awareness intensifies, so does the amount of time spent in "true meditation," resulting in more yang chi being cultivated during each session. This means that the rate at which the LDT fills up actually accelerates with continual practice. Eventually, when reaching a state of continual conscious awareness beyond the mind, accomplishing level one can be achieved in less than a week.

Level one takes an estimated five hundred hours of normal meditation or eighty hours of "focused concentration" meditation (also referred to as true meditation). Looking back, it took Jim ten years to complete level one, but he began training in five to ten minute intervals initially.[10] It took John Chang five years to complete level one. However, it is very possible that Liao Che Tung attained level one in only a few months.[11]

The rate at which a practitioner makes progress in any energy cultivation practice also depends on his/her age and his/her current health. The energy distributes less efficiently based on these aspects. However, a person's willingness to commit and practice every day is the single most important factor in determining success in energy cultivation and can easily outweigh the other factors.

Many cultivation schools recommend practicing forty-five minutes twice a day to make effective progress, and some even train up to four hours per day. Increasing the time spent training can accelerate one's growth, but only if the practitioner can keep his/her life in balance. If one's outer life is not stable then they will have no ability to quiet their mind and achieve a quality meditative state. The key is to fight both the outer battle and the inner battle. Looking at John Chang, he progressed rather steadily through a long period of time, becoming successful both outwardly and inwardly.

The Lower Dantien

The lower dantien is an organ on the etheric body made of tissue that acts as a container with the function of storing and refining the yang chi. Filling the LDT is often referred to as "building the foundation." This is because the lower dantien serves as the foundation for supplying the force behind a person's capability to purify the energy centers along the spine. In esoteric terms the capacity of the lower dantien is literally the strength of a person's Kundalini. Therefore, the lower dantien plays an important role with regards to purifying and activating the etheric body. In this regard, the lower dantien is similar to the engine inside of a car. Many traditions including the Shaolin monks understand this and also begin their internal training with lower dantien breathing very similar to the Mo Pai method.

Mo Pai limits the breathing to the stomach area in order to focus exclusively on filling the lower dantien with yang chi. As such, when focusing exclusively on the lower dantien, it becomes filled at a faster pace. Natural breathing fills all three dantiens, but at a slower pace. Mo Pai focuses on filling the lower dantien exclusively because the later training leading up to fusion is not concerned with the middle and upper dantien. Mo Pai training takes a different route towards nirvana, not concerned with climbing the ladder of chakras, and instead makes an effort to combine the two energies (yang chi and yin chi) inside of the lower dantien.

Horse Stance Posture

Besides meditation practice, is also important that the level one practitioner train the horse stance on a regular bases.

The horse stance is a very popular training method in almost all energy cultivation systems and martial arts throughout China. In regards to energy practice, many masters teach that horse stance focuses the energy in the lower dantien, preventing it from "leaking" to other areas of the body and allowing a practitioner to ascend at an accelerated pace.

Note: The notion of preventing the "leaking" of energy is also associated with the "full lotus" sitting posture.

From a physical perspective, the horse stance predominantly strengthens the lower body. As weight lifters will explain, the lower body is connected with one's testosterone levels. For this reason, it is easy to understand why the secret for many body builders is actually in their leg training. With higher testosterone levels an individual is able to put on heavy amounts of muscle mass in a shorter period of time. The elixir, "jing," the first dantien is known as vitality. This is because the first dantien has a direct correlation with the physical body and will be cultivated in tandem with a stronger and healthier body. Secondly, increasing one's connection with their body also enhances meditation practice. Considering the trinity of mind, body, and spirit, when one is working with their body they are increasing their control over the mind and allowing themselves to cultivate spirit.

Sensations

Throughout the Mo Pai levels many sensations arise that can serve as a road map during the different stages of progression.

Heat in the lower dantien is an important sensation that will occur. The heat will grow and grow as one progresses. Eventually at the end of level one, the heat will be so intense that it will be at a point of feeling like there is lava inside one's stomach. Just by physically pumping the lower stomach muscles in and out, one will be able to create a feeling of intense heat. This is because when a practitioner quickly and continuously pulls the lower stomach in and out, they are also moving the yang chi inside of the lower dantien and creating friction. The friction between the moving yang chi creates heat.[12]

It is very important to note the connection between the physical and the subtle. The physical movements are affecting the yang chi in the etheric body. *By moving the physical body, one is also causing movements of the yang chi in the lower dantien.* A practitioner's physical body is interlayered with their etheric body, making this possible.

The sensation of heat is seen as a sign of progression in Mo Pai, but it is fundamentally a warning sign from the body. This sensation is telling the student that their dantien is at a high capacity. Meaning they are about ready for level two. Anyone who is at this point needs to be extremely careful not to break the seventy-two-hour rule so that they can avoid rupturing their dantien. The extreme lava-like sensation that develops is even more unnatural for the body and is a warning sign that the dantien is at an alarming capacity.

The second sensation that occurs during level one is "vibrations." This is noted to be the last sensation experienced during level one. However, Jim McMillan mentions that this sensation only lasts for a short time and then goes away forever.[13] Vibrations have to do with activating the lower dantien and will be covered in more detail in further sections.

The 72-Hour Rule

The 72 Hour Rule states that if one has any type of orgasm and expels semen, that they must stop training entirely for three days (seventy-two hours). If one does not heed this warning and trains with focused concentration during the seventy-two-hour time period, then they will become at serious risk of tearing their lower dantien. The danger for rupture arises because after one has had an orgasm, the lower dantien becomes sealed and the body goes into a state of recovery in an effort to regain the vital-energy spent.

Towards the end of level one and the start of level two,

the Mo Pai practitioner begins to cultivate yang chi in the LDT beyond one-hundred percent capacity. It is this abnormal level of yang chi accumulated inside of a Mo Pai practitioner's lower dantien that creates the risk for rupture when the seventy-two-hour rule is broken. The sensation of heat is the best indication of risk level.

This injury ends one's training. As mentioned earlier, the lower dantien serves as an important container for the practitioner's yang chi, and a torn container (ruptured lower dantien) cannot be filled. Further training only agitates the injury, and not even John Chang himself is confident when it comes to healing this injury.

When considering that the amount of energy inside of the LDT is an important factor for determining how quickly or slowly a person progresses in awakening his/her chakras. From the perspective of spiritual growth, it is easy to understand why the LDT rupture is such a catastrophic liability. If a person ruptures his or her dantien they not only lose the ability to gain power, but it also hinders their ability to ascend consciously. Respecting the 72 Hour Rule is a very substantial aspect of Mo Pai training.

Level Two

FORMING THE MASS

Training Overview

The practitioner entering the level two training has filled their lower dantien (LDT) with yang chi to one-hundred percent capacity through the meditation training in level one. Now the purpose of the second level is for the student to *compress and compact* the yang chi currently residing inside of the LDT, and also to continue the meditation practice in order to *accumulate more* yang chi in the LDT. Through a persistent practice of compressing and accumulating yang chi in the dantien, the final goal of the level two training is to eventually increase the amount of yang chi inside of the LDT to *twice the normal capacity*.

In the level two training, the student is practicing both the previous meditation technique and also the level two horse stance exercise. Below is an analysis of the level two horse stance exercise that highlights the important aspects involved, allowing readers to assimilate an understanding of the underlying mechanics.[*]

Level Two Exercise

The level two isometrics exercise begins with the practitioner positioned in a wide horse stance. The stance does not have to be extremely low and can be comfortable. While in horse stance position, the arms are stretched out in front of the practitioner. The exercise begins with pulling the arms back and rotating them as if pulling an imaginary rope, while at the same time tensing the muscles associated with the movement as if pulling something very heavy.

The practitioner needs to make sure that all of the muscles **not** involved in the pulling are relaxed. Most importantly, *the muscles involved with breathing are to be relaxed.* It is essential that the breath should be in control and relaxed. This is important to avoid lung problems and breathing conditions. One should also make sure not to focus on tensing the legs, and to only tense the muscles involved with the pulling.

When the practitioner has fully breathed in and the arms are at the practitioner's sides, they then hold their breath for ten to fifteen seconds while still maintaining tension in the muscles. During this time they focus their chi in the lower dantien. Now still continuing to maintain the tension, the practitioner pushes their arms forward, moving slowly, as if pushing an imaginary wall. Remaining in horse stance, the student is ready to repeat the exercise. This is an outline of the level two training.

Moderation

The level two exercise is to be done in moderation. This exercise is very physically taxing.[1] A person could get a hernia or other physical illnesses if the practitioner does more than 5 repetitions per session during the first few months. The body needs to gradually become more comfortable with the exercise. Be aware, many students practicing the level two technique have reported prostate related problems, ruptured veins, and breathing problems while doing the pushing exercise. In most cases, stopping the training reverses the negative effects on the body.

Horse Stance Continued

As mentioned previously, a correct horse stance will focus the practitioner's chi in the lower dantien area, preventing the chi from spreading down the legs. Often times, however, practitioners perform the horse stance posture incorrectly. If the practitioner performs horse stance improperly, then the chi will be not be stored in the lower dantien rendering it ineffective.

The Chinese refer to a correct horse stance posture as having "dawn." This means that the practitioner should not be drooping and relying on the legs to hold the posture. Instead, to achieve "dawn," the focus of the posture should be centered at the lower dantien area and the legs should not be using all of the force to hold the person up. A person with "dawn" is stable and solid. "Dawn" is best taught on a personal basis by martial artists who have trained extensively in China. Master He Jing-han explains how to achieve "dawn" properly in his free instructional online videos. He explains horse stance and its importance in relation to "dawn", which allows the practitioner to store energy in the lower dantien.[2]

Proper horse stance position serves to isolate yang chi into the lower dantien area. The pressing and tensing movements contained in the level two exercise serve to press and compact the yang chi. By isolating the yang chi, then pressing and condensing it, the yang chi in the LDT is being formed together and becoming denser. Over time, this process creates a *hardened mass* of yang chi, which continues to grow in size as the training is repeated.

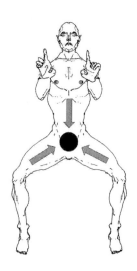

Horse Stance - Yang Chi Isolation

Overview

John Chang gives a powerful summary of the level two training when he says the following:

> "Then, for Level 2, we compress the yang chi and actually introduce twice as much into the same area. We make it hard so to speak."[3]

The important aspect is that in level two the student is *compressing* the yang chi together and hardening it. By compressing the yang chi and making it hardened, the practitioner is able to introduce twice as much yang chi into the lower dantien. By isolating the flow of yang chi in the dantien and also pressing it together, the individual is creating a blockage, or a "hardened" mass of yang chi. This hardened yang chi mass inside of the LDT is cultivated to a specific size so that the lower dantien contains twice its normal capacity of yang chi.

Level 1 - 100% Full   Level 2 - 200% Full

The second part of the training is the level one meditation technique. The meditation technique serves to accumulate more yang chi into the lower dantien in order to fill vacant space that is being created when condensing the yang chi. So, in this training one is "packing" the yang chi already stored in the LDT, and then accumulating more yang chi to fill its place. This process of condensing and gathering yang chi repeats until the mass is cultivated to the correct specifications and the LDT is holding 2X its normal capacity.

It is easy to see how accumulating this much yang chi in the lower dantien can become dangerous for a practitioner's etheric composition. On the opposite side of the spectrum, considering the practitioner will have twice as much yang chi as a normal human, they also have the capacity to seriously injure others.[4]

The practitioner at this point has a full dantien with a large condensed yang chi mass residing inside. After level two, the student is at the highest level of yang chi accumulation.[5] The next two levels have to do with manipulating and fusing the energy gathered in level one and two.

There are sensations, but for the most part, the student knows when level two is complete based on a teacher's guidance and evaluation. For someone that does not have a teacher, they will need to train their awareness sufficiently before approaching level two. Unless they have attained the capacity to feel and manipulate chi, judging the extent that they have progressed in level two would be like walking around in the dark.

It is theoretically possible that one can get a rough estimate of how big the "mass" should be at the end of level two based on the relative size of the lower dantien. However, beyond such speculation, others may have also provided a few clues as to the size of a fully developed yang chi mass.

> "...the dantien is no bigger than the tip of your pinky finger all shriveled up when you first begin training. The other x-ray was more dramatic. It showed the dantien (John's) in a fully developed condition. It was about the size of a 50-cent piece and solid."
>
> -Jim McMillan[6]

While it is misleading, this quote actually explains how the fully developed chi yang mass will be about the size of a 50-cent piece at the end of the level two training. The quote is referring to the size of the dantien, but this is a misunderstanding that will be discussed in detail in the next chapter. For now, note that in the quote it is being described as a solid. Also, understand that the mass is being described in the quote as "the size of a 50-cent piece." This theoretically makes sense for the size that a fully developed yang chi mass should be when considering what size it would need to be in order to increase an average-sized lower dantien to two-hundred percent capacity.

Blockage Information

John Chang explains how in level two the student is actually, "shaping the chi to the correct specifications."[9]

The mass of yang chi inside of the LDT has to be cultivated to a specific size in order for a true level four fusion to occur. As mentioned, a master should be present during this training, as it would be very hard to tell if the level two mass was cultivated either too small or too large.

The level two practitioner is compacting chi inside of the dantien to the point of creating a solid "mass." This mass of chi is what many Qi Gong doctors refer to as a "blockage."

> "...people's chi can become stagnant or it can completely block your body's meridians. When this happens it can and will cause illness. Your chi needs to move through the meridians unobstructed in order to ward off illness and keep you healthy."
>
> -Jim McMillan[10]

In the average individual whose yang chi stagnates and develops blockages, this over time creates illness in the physical body. A respectable Qi Gong doctor will work to free the blockages that are suspended in the meridians, in turn improving the flow of the patient's vital energy. By healing the patient's etheric body the doctor is producing healing to the physical body as well. Opening chakras and activating the etheric body is a method for a person to self-clean and refine their own energy system.

If compressed in the same area, one's yang chi will clump together and form a mass. Very similar to how stagnant blood clots together. This is how energy blockages are formed. In individuals who suffer from a degree of stagnation, whether it be physical or awareness based, their yang chi stops flowing effectively and eventually begins to clump together. A consistency of non-circulating yang chi clots together and creates masses.

The phenomenon of yang chi coagulating is not an unfamiliar phenomenon in Chinese cultivation. Qi Gong doctors have termed these yang chi masses using the word "blockages," because of their nature to restrict the natural flow of chi in the body. Considering the blockage is made of chi, it is understandable the degree that it can block healthy flowing chi. For this reason, blockages normally have a negative connotation to them. Similar to the yin-yang symbol that reflects light in darkness, Mo Pai cultivators intentionally compact their yang chi to create a blockage, or "hardened mass," in order to store twice the normal amount of chi in the lower dantien.

GATES – The Lower Dantien

A large portion of the level two training focuses entirely on compacting yang chi inside the dantien into a hardened mass, thus increasing the amount of yang chi that can be accumulated inside of one's dantien beyond the normal limits.

When referring to compressing yang chi inside of the lower dantien in order to store twice as much yang chi into the dantien, John Chang says, "You must be sexually abstinent to complete this training."[7]

The reason that the practitioner must be sexually abstinent during the Mo Pai training, and most importantly during the yang chi compression involved in the level two training, is so that the practitioner's chi has access to the lower dantien. Without abstinence from sex, the lower dantien will become inaccessible and therefor will not be cultivated, rendering the training useless.

When referring to the level two training, John Chang makes a point to say that sexual abstinence keeps, "the gates of the dantien open."[8]

The practitioner would need to remain abstinent from sex so that the gates of the dantien stay open, allowing the yang chi to be able to enter the lower dantien. As explained, if the practitioner does not remain abstinent then the lower dantien will become closed, or sealed, and the yang chi will not be able to accumulate in the lower dantien. Therefore, abstinence is important both for the accumulation of yang chi as well as the "hardening" involved in level two.

Level Two Sensations

The excessive amount of yang chi being stored in the LDT as result of the level two training causes the energy channels in the body to become more active.

When the LDT is filled past normal capacity, it causes excessive yang chi to continuously flow through the limbs. The yang chi in the LDT moves up to the heart area and then moves out through the channels in the arms or can be directed to the head.[11] As a result, the student experiences the energy channels in the arms and the energy points in the hands to open at an accelerated rate. This is commonly followed by the sensation of heat in the palms.[12] The energy points being referred to in the palms of the hands are also known as chakras. Whenever an energy point/chakra is being opened, there is a sensation of heat associated with it.

Without the Mo Pai training, there exists a method attributed to the ancient Egyptians that is effective for directly opening the energy centers in the palms. Besides projecting chi, the Egyptians believe opening the energy points in the hands is also important for allowing one to become able to heal others. (John Chang also notes this aspect of healing on pg. 218 of McMillan's book)

The Egyptian exercise is done in seven second intervals, with a one second pause in between each motion. Begin with the left hand palm facing up and the right hand on top of the left hand palm facing down. Begin inhaling slowly for seven seconds and at the same time rubbing the left hand (fingers included) with the right hand in a circular motion from right to left. Then flip the left hand over and do the same circular motion while exhaling for seven seconds. Do the same for the right hand, but rotate the left hand in a circular motion from left to right.[13]

Testing

The testing for level two involves the student pushing his yang chi from the LDT through the arms and shooting the chi out of the palms all in one motion. With the help of John Chang's yin field, the student is able to knock down objects from a distance. John Chang's yin field is important so that the student's yang chi is able to leave his/her body and make contact with an object. Related feats have been performed by Jim McMillan and can be seen on YouTube.

72-Hour Rule – DANGER STARTS

The seventy-two-hour rule becomes *more significant* as one progresses in the level two training. This is because at this stage the lower dantien is being cultivated to unnatural levels of yang chi. Normal systems of conscious evolution, or immortality, move past the dantien at this point and do not continue to cultivate the dantien further. As such, they do not have a "72 hour-rule." Tearing the lower dantien is not a problem or hazard for these other schools. Mo Pai has created this problem because the practitioner is now condensing yang chi inside of the lower dantien, resulting it being filled past its normal capacity. As the lower dantien is being supplied an unnatural and dangerous amount of yang chi it becomes at risk of popping if handled improperly. It would seem that obeying the seventy-two hour rule would be fundamental, but many students deep in training are actually quick to ignore this rule.

Once a student begins level two, John Chang can no longer protect them. This is because John Chang is not able to heal this injury with one-hundred percent success. Healing of an injury of this magnitude depends on the student. In most cases, the student will be permanently done with Mo Pai. If one's dantien becomes ruptured, besides the fact that the individual will not be able to hold large amounts of yang chi, further training for them will only agitate the injury.

Level Two Seated Training

It is necessary to mention that a technique once surfaced proposing the possibility to perform the level two training from a purely seated position. However, it is important to note that Jim McMillan, who completed level two and progressed to level three, did not mention practicing this seated form to his students.

The idea behind this theoretical seated training is that one can compress yang chi inside of the lower dantien by closing off the dantien and then pumping the stomach inward. Closing off the LDT is done by sitting in lotus or half lotus and then pulling up the anus and genitals as if one was trying to keep from going to the bathroom (this prevents yang chi from escaping/transforming by closing the Hui Yin point). After that, one continually pumps in their stomach muscles, so as to "compress" the yang chi.[14, 15] There is no heavy tensing involved in this exercise, but one is holding their breath.

What is interesting though, is that the exercise may have some significance because one of the westerners who was practicing this method, before the horse stance method was released publically, reached out for help after having ruptured their dantien. *The dantien rupture can only occur if one is condensing chi,* which results in pressuring the lower dantien beyond its normal capacity.

This exercise is only being mentioned as an interesting alternative to the practices released by the official western students, and while I may personally believe it could have significance, the technique should not be regarded highly.

Level Three
HANDLING THE POWER

The level three Mo Pai training brings a lot of confusion to practitioners because of a few key misunderstandings surrounding the internal mechanics of the practice. The main importance is understanding what has been done in the training so far and what is going on in the practices to come.

In the texts provided, both Jim McMillan and Kosta Danaos explain that during the level three training it is **the lower dantien** that the student is freeing from the cords that keep it in place. **This is not correct**. There is a slight mix-up. In both texts, they write that in level three the student is "freeing" the lower dantien from the "cords" keeping it in place. However, it is not the lower dantien that the student is dealing with in level three.

To gain an understanding of what is going on in level three it is important to take a step back. Looking back, in level two, the practitioner is compacting the yang chi inside his/her lower dantien through consistent training of the Mo Pai level two horse stance exercise. The goal of this training was to create a solid mass of yang chi to a size of correct specifications.

Now, the confusion comes about because in level three the students are told that they now have to work with the dantien as a whole and free it from the cords keeping it in place. However, it is not the dantien that the student is freeing from the cords. **The practitioner is actually freeing the "yang chi mass" that was cultivated in the level two training from the cords keeping it in place.** It is the hardened yang chi mass formed in level two that the practitioner is concerned with in level three and not the lower dantien. For clarification, this yang chi mass is located *inside* of the dantien, and is not the dantien itself.

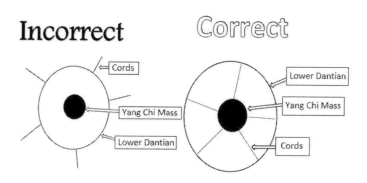

The student at level three is not making the entire dantien with a yang chi mass inside of it mobile. In the level three training, the student is simply making the yang chi mass mobile.

It is the same mass that was created in level two that is

now the focus of the level three training. No new mass is introduced. One does not build a lower dantien or make it compact. To disregard the yang chi mass created in level two would neglect the purpose of the level two training. The very reason that the original Mo Pai levels are referred to as 1, 2a, 2b, 3, is because level 2b is dealing with the same yang chi mass cultivated in level 2a. Level 2b is the second part of level 2a. Level 2a builds and hardens the yang chi mass, and level 2b frees the yang chi mass from the cords holding it in place. Going further, the next level converts the yang chi mass to yin chi in order to prepare for fusion. When describing the levels, this book uses the simplified version (1, 2, 3, 4) that John Chang taught to his western students. This is done in order to stay consistent with the texts provided by the western students, primarily Jim McMillan and Kosta Danaos.

To put the level three training situation in perspective, all humans have a lower dantien within their etheric body, regardless of their background with energy cultivation. The lower dantien existed before the development of Mo Pai because it has a fundamental role to play in the human system. The LDT is a location where the etheric body refines and stores the vital energy. This energy is known as jing in Taoist alchemy and referred to as chi in Mo Pai. It is the vital substance one is constantly absorbing from the sun, food, and air around them. This natural process is paramount to every human beings development and health, for it to be disrupted would be catastrophic. Ultimately, a human's goal is to refine the lower energies in order to attain the higher and more subtle energies. This is the purpose of Daoist alchemy, the cultivation of jing to chi, and chi to shen, and finally shen to ling/wuji. For this reason, the lower dantien is paramount for an individual's conscious development towards being able to experience reality as it truly is (awakening/enlightenment).

Due to the fundamental role that the LDT plays towards one's existence, it cannot be compacted or relocated as one desires without serious implications. The LDT rupture is an injury that is serious enough, as outlined by John Chang. To actually relocate the LDT would be similar to moving one's liver around their stomach, or compressing one's liver.

Controlling the Chi Mass

John Chang teaches that the chi outside of our body is in an "undisciplined state."[1]

When chi is absorbed, it changes into a docile state, allowing it to be controlled by the student. The yang chi has become an extension of oneself once it is absorbed and become docile to the practitioner's will. Mo Pai nei kung involves manipulating large masses of this life-force with one's consciousness. The idea of manipulating large masses of chi gives tremendous insight into level three, because in this level the student is removing the mass from the cords keeping it in place.

"They (great masters) are using energy and they are using their mind to control it."[2]

–Kosta Danaos

The mind/awareness is the key to controlling chi. The "dantien" in level three is actually the mass of hardened yang chi cultivated in level two. Due to this, the practitioner has the ability to move the mass at will around his/her body. After the mass has been freed from the cords that keep it in place, the mass becomes mobile and the practitioner can use his/her mind/awareness to manipulate it. By manipulating the mass of yang chi, the practitioner is able to perform various training functions.

Martial Arts Master

Kosta Danaos provides an example of his friend in Greece who was a Korean martial arts master and practitioner of nei kung who would perform feats of super human strength. This master had a solid mass in his stomach at the dantien point that he could manipulate at will. Upon examination of the mass, the doctor physically felt a lump that the martial arts master could manipulate at will.[3]

This same man depicted in the story Kosta Danaos presented to John Chang has cultivated a mass of hardened yang chi and freed it from the "cords" that hold it in place The martial artist has attained what is required in the level three training of the Mo Pai system.

In response to Danaos's story, John Chang confirmed the connection with level three when saying, "It is the same for us, this man is at least level 3."

John Chang also goes on to describe the phenomenon further when saying, "Yes, it is a solid lump of hardened yang chi he can tap into and use at will."[4]

Here, John Chang is confirming the connection between the mass in the martial artist's body and the Mo Pai level three training. Here, John Chang is defining the purported "dantien" used in level three, and making it clear that it is actually a hardened mass of yang chi.

Also, a remarkable aspect about this story is that when the martial artist moves the yang chi mass around his stomach there is a noticeable physical distortion in the occurrence of a "lump". The actual yang chi mass contained in the etheric body is causing distortions on the physical body. This phenomenon is similar to what Kosta Danaos presented about yin chi. He described how when yin chi is absorbed while training meditation, it will cause a wet spot to form under the practitioner. The frequency of the subtle energies (yang chi/yin chi) are interfering and affecting the physical frequency of matter. This gives insight into the dramatic capabilities that Nei Gong training can provide. Similar to the many stories of vaporizing matter or pressing chopsticks through tables. The capabilities are endless as one goes deeper. John Chang himself is a scientist working on the metaphysical plane. It is like Neo in *The Matrix* who while getting shot at does not need to block or dodge the bullets because he has a deeper connection with reality, instead he just makes the bullets stop in midair.

Coming back to the story, it is clear that the martial artist moves this mass with his awareness/mind and is not using any limbs, devices, or any particular exercise.

The yang chi mass is literally an extension of the

martial artist's consciousness. This is because the chi is *docile* to the practitioner's will once it has been absorbed. John Chang mentions yang chi in the air around us as energy that isn't docile or controllable, but then becomes under our command when we absorb it.

> "Chi comes from all around us, it is pulled from its natural undisciplined state from both earth (yin) and sky (yang)."

> –John Chang[5]

The only aspect that most practitioners lack is the awareness of the chi energy, which has to be gained before one can manipulate the chi. However, this comes quickly with continual meditation practice. Only after the chi has been gathered and one gains an awareness of it will the practitioner become able to control it with their mind. Once the yang chi mass is unbound through the level three exercises, the practitioner will be able to move this mass of yang chi at will using his/her mind just as if moving an arm or a leg. The reason the martial artist is able to move the mass around at will is because the chi has been absorbed, and naturally become docile, allowing it to be manipulated with the mind. When one feels the chi, they move the chi through feeling using the mind/awareness, just as if moving an arm or a leg. It is as if the thought of moving one's chi becomes a familiar feeling.

On a side note, since ancient times Buddhists have

taught people to be aware of not only ones actions, but also one's thoughts. This teaching has esoteric connections because one's thoughts carries one's energy. Also, if John Chang teaches that karma has to do not only with one's actions but also one's thoughts. Often times, people can feel it when others have negative thoughts towards them.

The main focus in the level three training is for the practitioner to remove the yang chi mass from the "cords" that keep it in place in order to set the necessary preparations for level four.

John Chang says that after one has severed the connections, then they are able to move the dantien (yang chi mass) around freely.

> "In level 3 we make the dantien (yang chi mass) mobile, we can make it move."[6]

The goal of the level three training is to sever the connections so that the yang chi mass can be moved around at will. After becoming completely disconnected, the student has "control" over the yang chi mass.

During the training process, as the yang chi mass becomes more and more disconnected through continual practice, it also begins to move around the stomach freely and cause noticeable distortions on the physical body.

"Supposed to occur at the end of level 3. When the dantien becomes disconnected (partially disconnected) it would be illustrated by a <u>small bulging under the skin</u> on the right side. You will actually see it move a couple of inches under your skin toward the dantien and stop there. He then demonstrated this for me by <u>placing his finger</u> under his shirt, pushing it outward slightly and moving it across a short distance."[7]

-Jim McMillian

The yang chi mass in the etheric body distorts the physical body causing a lump. This lump can be moved by the mind, like the martial artist does, because the lump is actually caused by a dense mass consisting of matter on a higher frequency. This is a phenomenon where the lump that moves on the physical body is entirely caused by something "non-physical."

The extent that the physical lump appears, also gives notion to the actual size of the blockage/mass that needs to be cultivated. If a lump does not appear, then the practitioner has not cultivated the mass to a large enough size. Many times there is confusion because students think it is their dantien they are manipulating, so they believe it does not need to be cultivated to correct specifications (even though this was clearly outlined in level two). Only when one understands that it is actually a mass of yang chi does it become understandable that the mass could have been cultivated too small. If the mass is too small, then there will be problems with the level four fusion.

It is important to note that John Chang has to demonstrate the physical distortion that will occur near the end of level three by moving his finger under his shirt. John Chang no longer has a solid mass of yang chi in his body because he transformed it into yin energy at the beginning of level four by sending it to his perineum (Hui Yin). John Chang still has his dantien though, which is used to "house" the two yin and yang energies for the fusion process in level four.

After the yang chi mass is free from the cords that hold it in place, the practitioner can move this blockage, or mass of yang chi, around their body at will. Because of this, once free, the yang chi mass can be utilized for more functions than simply preparing for the level four fusion. John Chang teaches that the mass can actually be manipulated to perform various methods of training.[8]

To understand this training method first realize that when a student has freed the yang chi mass from the cords holding it in place, that they are then able to move mass freely around their body. This is similar to the martial artist who would pass his cultivated chi mass into his arms and legs. The Mo Pai practitioner does the same, but with the purpose of dislocating other blockages, or small "masses," and removing stagnant chi in their meridians. By removing stagnant debris and blockages the practitioner will increase his/her energy flow and in turn open the meridians as well as the energy points, or chakras, in the arms and legs. This technique is a powerful method to quickly activate one's body, as normally the body does not become activated until the central channel, sushumna, has been activated. This technique is using a blockage to clear multiple blockages. Similar to cutting diamonds with a diamond saw. Finally, after clearing the body, the practitioner returns the yang chi mass back inside his/her lower dantien.

When the student reaches a certain level of awareness they become conscious of the chi masses or blockages that are not only residing within them but also within others. With this awareness they can manipulate the masses and clear meridians both in themselves and others. This is a common practice by authentic qi gong doctors.

X-Rays

There is a section where Jim McMillan describes John Chang showing him two separate X-rays of the dantien area. One x-ray is of John Chang's dantien and the other is of a students. Both x-rays show a yang chi mass, misclassified as the dantien itself, standing out clearly. When shown the x-rays, Jim McMillan's becomes concerned is that what he believes is the "dantien" in each of the photos is visible. Jim McMillan suspects that the x ray photos may were doctored by John Chang to illustrate a point because western scientists would have surely seen the dantiens of normal individuals during examinations in the past. And if so, many scientists would have surely conducted extensive research into determining what the masses were.[9]

The error, however, is that the "dantiens" depicted in the x-rays are actually the yang chi masses that were cultivated and repeatedly condensed and hardened through the level two Mo Pai training. The x-rays of the Mo Pai practitioners are depicting a spectacle that is only cultivated through the training itself, and is not a natural phenomenon. Therefore, normal individuals who do not train Mo Pai will not have a mass depicted when x-rayed.

These large and repeatedly hardened masses appear on the x-ray because they affect and interact with physical matter. From the martial arts demonstration, John Chang's level three instructions, the level 1 heat, and the yin chi "wet spot," it is clear that the large yang chi mass, even though not on the physical frequency, has the capability to distort the physical and affect an x-ray.

The two different x-rays shown to Jim McMillan each depict a different size yang chi mass. The first is very small and the second, that of John Chang's, is much larger. The two masses are different sizes because the mass grows in size as it is cultivated through consistent training of the level two technique.

> "X-Rays show that the dantien is no bigger than the tip of pinky finger all shriveled up when you first begin training. The other x-ray was more dramatic, it showed the dantien (John Chang's) in a fully developed condition; it was about the size of a 50-cent piece and solid."

> –Jim McMillan[10]

The x-rays that John Chang is showing to Jim McMillan are from the past, he no longer has a mass in his dantien. The yang chi mass goes away after level four. This is why John Chang has to use his finger under his shirt in order to demonstrate to McMillan the lump that will appear because of the yang chi mass being freed from the cords holding it in place.

"Cords"

For many students of Mo Pai, the nature of the "cords" that keep the yang chi mass in place is a mystery. The cords were not explained thoroughly and are for the most part a mystery to the practitioners of the system. Surely one would be wise to question what exactly they are breaking during this training, and what the resulting implications to the etheric body are from such an act.

Luckily, many experienced masters in the past can help give insight into this process. The truth is that there are no implications for breaking the cords that hold the mass in place. These "cords" hold no practical value to the practitioner's energy body, and are extraneous in nature.

To put the situation in perspective, the body of the average human can slowly accumulate stagnate debris of yang chi. This debris eventually accumulates and forms blockages of yang chi. This is mostly due to a lack of physical activity or awareness-based exercise (any form of concentration), resulting in one's chi circulation to not be sufficient and stagnate. As discussed, this stagnant chi causes physical illness over time, and it is the purpose of trained medical qi gong doctors to either remove the blockages or dissolve them entirely. The process of removing these blockages causes a person's chi to flow more efficiently, making them feel much better physically, emotionally, and mentally, often within only a few minutes after the treatment. In the patient's etheric body, the blockages keep themselves suspended in the meridians (channels) by cords that grow and attach themselves to the walls of the energy channels. These "cords" keep the blockages suspended in the patient's body, resulting in blocked energy flow to a particular area.

It is important to remember that the chi energy is very much **alive,** the chi mass cultivated in level two is not a dead solid, but a living and growing mass. The chi being compacted is literally a form of life force. In Mo Pai, the practitioner is intentionally cultivating a colossal sized blockage over the continual compression of yang chi involved in the isometric exercise of level two. The cords are entirely a growth of this mass and are of no importance to the energy body, they are to be viewed as debris and can be cut or removed without harm.

Level Three Training Overview

Once the yang chi mass has been cultivated from consistent level two training, the question becomes how does one free the mass from the "cords" that hold it in place? The official Mo Pai level three exercise is unknown to most westerners, and is only partially accessible to students directly under Jim McMillan. As time passes, however, it is possible that level three will spill from either a top student of Jim McMillan or possibly even an Indonesian student. Astrologers would say that the human race is currently in the age of information, a time when the unknown comes to the surface.

The goal in level three is to free the yang chi mass cultivated in level two from the bondages, or "cords", that hold it in place. The practitioner is to allow the yang chi mass to become completely mobile.

Previously, John Chang talked about making the dantien (yang chi mass) mobile so that the practitioner can move it around at will, and in order to make it mobile, he/she must first break the cords that are holding it in place.

> "We move it in these four directions first, like an X, after that we can make the dantien move anywhere."[11]
>
> –John Chang

Jim McMillan also describes level three as a "physical movement" which during the exercise involves moving the right hand and feeling "prick sensations."[12]

Using this information, it is possible to understand that level three involves moving the yang chi mass in an x-fashion by physically moving the right hand. A physical movement is being used in order to displace the yang chi mass.

Looking back at Kosta's martial artist story, there is a practitioner who can move the level three yang chi mass around their stomach at will, causing distortions on the physical body in the form of a "lump." Considering from the martial arts example, and John Chang's finger under his shirt example, it is reasonable to say that the yang chi mass can cause distortions on the physical plane. It is also understandable that physical movements themselves can also cause distortions on the etheric body. For example, when the level one practitioner pumps his/her stomach in and out, they are using a physical movement to cause the yang chi inside of the lower dantien to move around and create friction, resulting in the sensation of heat.

Similarly, if a level three student is using their physical hand to press and move the area of their lower stomach where the LDT resides, then they will also be moving the yang chi mass in the dantien of the etheric body. Over time through a process of moving the mass in an x-fashion it will become possible to break the mass free from the cords holding it in place.

Qi Gong masters often look strange rubbing their arms and legs with their hands, as if taking a shower in the middle of an open field on a sunny day. In fact, these masters are performing this exercise because the physical movements are causing an interaction with the etheric body by which a clearing of the chi channels takes place, creating space for an increase in the flow of energy within the etheric body.

There is also another theoretical way for one to approach level three. Through meditation practice if the student is able to achieve an awareness of the yang mass, they can then use their mind to move the yang chi mass in the x-formation. This may be difficult however. An awareness of the energy body and the blockages inside of it comes with continual meditation practice, but once aware, the practitioner soon finds they have control of the chi also. Similar to Kosta Danaos's martial artist, the student can move the mass with their mind. By moving the mass in the x-shape formation repeatedly, and on a continual basis, theoretically they can eventually break it free from the "cords" that hold it in place.

Sensations

Jim McMillan describes an "electrical pricking sensation" while doing the level three physical exercise with his right hand, and he also mentions a "huge electric shock" he experienced twice during his training.[13] A theory for this, is that the level three practitioner, by doing the training, is actually moving the yang chi mass near his perineum and causing an electrical shock from the yin/yang interaction. In the *The Ring of Fire* documentary, while in the treatment room, John Chang explains that he consciously pulls the yang chi down from his solar plexus and the yin chi up from his perineum, and by doing so creates "an electric shock." Considering the yang chi mass is in the lower dantien, it is near the perineum and could be causing a similar reaction.

Concern

It is possible that there are implications for having a blockage this large inside of the human body. Readers should be aware that the Mo Pai practices can potentially be very damaging to the body.

> "Neikung is like taking steroids, it can go very bad, or it can go very good for a short amount of time."
>
> –Kosta Danaos[14]

Normally there is balance between the amount of yin chi and yang chi flowing in the etheric body, but when the yang chi becomes "hardened," the yang chi is not flowing. As such there is not a proportionate amount of yin chi flowing in the body. The mass increases the amount of yang chi, but causes an imbalance to yin chi. Until the practitioner brings the yang chi mass to the perineum in order to gather a proportionate amount of yin chi, there will be an imbalance. By holding onto this yang chi mass the practitioner is not only putting the lower dantien at risk, but is also preventing the energy system from gathering a proportionate amount of yin energy. A practitioner needs to be careful, because at this level they will have an overly-yang imbalance that can over time eventually cause inflammation in the yin-organs: primarily the kidneys, liver, and stomach.

Kidneys are the yin organ representing water in

Chinese medicine, they are the most affected from over-yang (fire) development.

Jim McMillan, who remained at level three for a long period of time, having never reached level four, was noted to have developed serious kidney related problems. However, most connect his illness to his time spent in the armed services and being exposed to "Agent Orange." It is somewhat startling to note that John Chang also developed kidney problems at one point and had to receive medical treatments.[15] Chang had already completed fusion at this time, so the two energies should have been in balance. But it is possible that his past training had a negative effect on his body. Regardless, I believe there is a connection between extensive yang chi cultivation and kidney problems. Being grounded and living in wet climates should benefit the avid Mo Pai practitioner.

Level Four

THE IMMORTAL SPARK

"The mundane is transformed in one clap of thunder."

-Lu Dogbin[1]

Level four involves fusing yin chi and yang chi inside of the student's lower dantien. Once complete, this allows the initiate to take their human characteristics with them after death (notably their yang chi). This fusion is considered to be of primary importance in the Mo Pai lineage, a type of graduation. If death occurs without fusion, one would simply become a low form of ghost without retaining their human characteristics.

The fusion process central to this stage in the training was the most difficult for the ancient masters to develop. It is said that many died trying to figure out the exact method for bringing the two energies together.[2] In the end, the founder of Mo Pai, Mo Tzu, was never successful in fusing the yin and yang energies together, and as such he was never able to be considered a true Mo Pai immortal. It was later down the line of students that level four was eventually successfully mastered.

The level four training consists of three primary

sections: generating yin chi, placing yin chi and yang chi inside of the lower dantien, and lastly fusing the two together. Once fused, the immortal lightning bolt is created inside one's being and they become a true Mo Pai master, capable of progressing further without any assistance.

The Training

Part One

The first part of Level four begins with sending the yang chi mass that was cultivated in the previous two levels down to the **Hui Yin acupuncture point,** located between the urinary tract and the anus. The Hui Yin point is a special point where the human body absorbs and accumulates yin chi. At the Hui Yin point, yin chi is gathered equal to the amount of yang chi that the practitioner sent down.[3] In this situation, the yang chi mass that was cultivated to a specific size is sent to down to Hui Yin in order to accumulate an equally proportionate amount of yin chi.

This amount of yin chi generated will be equal to the amount of yang chi that is currently being stored in the full dantien. Looking back, at the end of level two the practitioner had two times normal capacity of yang chi inside his/her dantien. This is because the dantien was full and also the student cultivated a condensed mass of the yang chi inside of the full dantien. Now that the yang chi mass has been lowered to the Hui Yin point, the dantien will again be at normal yang chi capacity and an equal amount of yin energy will be generated over time.

Part Two

Now after the yang chi mass has been lowered to the perineum to generate yin chi, John Chang says,

"Level 4 training the yin and yang rise together like this O O, they float around the body and the pain is incredible, constant, and unbelievable."[4]

Similar to the martial artist mentioned earlier, at this point the yin chi and yang chi are floating around the etheric body freely and causing disruptions to the physical body. The renegade energies are so powerful that their existence is interfering with the physical and being translated as incredible pain. This pain gives insight into the danger of this training and the implications if the practitioner is unable to fuse the two together.

John Chang says,

"If you have discipline to ignore the pain you can control them and put their power inside your dantien."[5]

The dantien continues to serve as a container just like in level one, but at this stage, it is used to store both yin chi and yang chi. In this case, the energies are floating around the body freely, and the practitioner must ignore the pain caused by the two and use his/her awareness to actually control the two and put them both inside of their lower dantien. This is similar to how the martial arts practitioner could control his yang chi mass with his awareness and move the physical distortions around his body.

John Chang says the following,

"The two forces repel each other and are not attracted."[6]

And,

"Bring yin and yang together, when level 4 is finished the two sit in dantien like this (S)"[7]

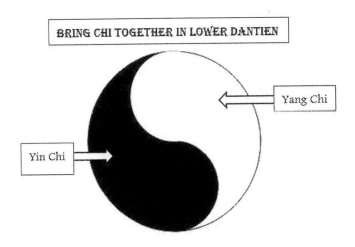

BRING CHI TOGETHER IN LOWER DANTIEN

Yang Chi

Yin Chi

When placed in the dantien, the yin and yang chi are still repelling each other and preventing fusion. As a result, they are together inside of the lower dantien in a fashion similar to oil inside of water. As such, this causes both of the energies to take up different locations in the lower dantien, forming a shape similar to the tai chi symbol. At this point the disciple will have succeeded in controlling and containing both the yin and yang chi inside of their lower dantien, but they have still not achieved fusion. *(Some would say that this is technically the end of level four, and level five is when the student actually merges the two together, but this detail can be disregarded.)*

Note: John Chang says that at this point in the level four training the yin chi and yang chi sit inside the dantien like a tai chi symbol. This reinforces the notion that the lower dantien is still the same container and is still intact for the level four training. The dantien is not the same as the chi mass that was condensed and hardened in level two and then manipulated in level three. The dantien is a container throughout the whole training process. The LDT is an organ of the etheric body and it does not disappear or change form during the training. This is because a functioning lower dantien is needed in order to survive. The LDT is important for each individual's health so that they can store and transform the vital energy obtained from their environment.

Part Three

The final process of the level four training is achieving fusion. When the two energies are inside of the lower dantien they are both residing in a fashion similar to the yin / yang symbol. This is because they are still repelling each other, creating a degree of separation and a lack of intermixing. The last step in the training is the most important, and that is to finally bring the two repelling energies together and cause them to react. In doing so, immortality is achieved and a new and more powerful "electric chi" is born.

Once the two energies are in the tai chi symbol position, the secret to getting them to come together is *silence*. Complete stillness of the mind is the key to the final phase of the level four training. It is silence which causes the two energies to come together and create the fusion. The individual must reach a state of total calm and silence of the mind. This is the secret that has evaded most seekers in the past.

In this final phase of his training, John Chang took extraordinary measures to complete this task. He went to the jungle and placed himself in an environment that would heighten his meditation practice with the goal of reaching complete stillness if the mind. *Note:* At this point in the training the yin chi and yang chi are resting inside the dantien.

"…to complete Level Four' I left my home and went into the jungle for a year. I did this in order to reach a state of total calm. I reverted

to the primitive, this is most important. Your
mind must be utterly still for yang and yin to
come together."[8]

–John Chang

John Chang simplified his lifestyle to a very primitive
one in order to assist with his level four training. John Chang
reverted to the primitive in order to reach a state of total calm.
The daily disturbances in his modern lifestyle were too
overwhelming for his mind and keeping him from reaching a
degree of complete silence. John Chang teaches that, "the mind
must be utterly still" for yin and yang to come together.

At this point the two energies inside of the lower
dantien (yin and yang) are still repelling each other and resting
in the tai chi position **(S)**. They will not come together unless the
practitioner is able to achieve a degree of complete mental
silence. If the practitioner is not able to achieve the degree of
complete mental silence necessary, then the two energies will
remain resting opposing each other in the tai chi formation.

John Chang says, "By forcing the
two together, you also force them to react."[9]

When the two energies come together they react. By
achieving complete mental silence, the individual is bridging
the gap between the two energies resting in the lower dantien,
and causing the two energies to come together and react. When

yin chi and yang chi react, the lightning bolt is created.

"The lightning bolt between the two is generated, and you begin to become as I am."[10]

By achieving complete mental silence and causing the two energies to merge together, one is creating the new electric qi and becoming an immortal like John Chang. This individual will be able to take their yang chi with them after death. The practitioner must achieve a state of concentration to such a degree that their awareness transcends their mind, thus reaching a state of silence. This degree of calm and silence is what is necessary for the practitioner to create the fusion between the two energies.

During this training, John Chang felt *sensations* while trying *multiple times* to fuse the yin/yang chi together.[11]

This circumstance of how it took John Chang several tries to achieve the degree of silence necessary for the two energies to completely fuse together gives valuable insight into the process. First, during his attempts at silence, he could feel that he was making progress and causing a reaction. This shows that the practitioner is actually given guidance that they are making a step in the right direction. Second, after each attempt, it is not over, and the energies continue to reside in the lower dantien awaiting the next attempt. John Chang was given multiple tries, meaning that the practitioner can practice and practice in order to become proficient at fusing the two.

What is the Secret to Silence?

The ancient masters knew that through silence one can complete the "great work," or the true purpose of alchemy, and attain the golden aura.

"Silence is golden."

Silence requires a higher degree of awareness and concentration. By concentrating and achieving silence, the individual is raising his/her energy. Or in other words, they are raising their kundalini and activating the lower dantien. By activating the lower dantien, one is creating a vortex inside of the lower dantien that causes the yin chi and yang chi to mix together. A master has to obtain a complete degree of mental silence in order for the dantien to be activated to a high enough degree to create a catalyst for fusion.

At the end of level one Jim McMillan describes his dantien as vibrating, but then the sensation went away forever.[12] This is the sensation associated with the dantien becoming activated. When the dantien is fully activated, the vortex inside of it is spinning at such a speed that the sensation of vibrations goes away. During meditation, by concentrating and achieving complete mental silence the practitioner is activating the lower dantien to a higher degree, and with both the yin and yang chi energies resting inside, it produces a fusion.

However, speeding up the vortex inside of the dantien during awareness/concentration-based meditation is also a double edged sword. If the gates are closed (72-hour rule), and the dantien is over 100% full, then a dantien rupture can result if one does meditation training and activates the dantien. The vortex will cause the sealed dantien to expand and detonate.

Extreme Difficulty

First, the disciple training level four must be able to handle the pain associated with the process of putting both of the energies inside of their lower dantien. Secondly, the disciple must also have the discipline and concentration strength to achieve total silence of the mind. These two aspects are what make level four the most difficult. John Chang cannot help his students in this regard; achieving fusion is left entirely to the student's determination. It is up to the student to master the mind, and no one can assist.[13]

Dangerous Nature

There is danger and even the possibility of death associated with the level four training.

When referring to the level four training, John Chang says, "If you are not successful then you will probably die."[14]

And,

Jim McMillan says, "Knowledge is best kept in secrecy it can actually be very dangerous if done improperly. People can become sick and/or die if they train incorrectly. Westerners training without instruction pay serious price."[15]

On one hand, if the student is not successful in bringing the two energies together inside of the lower dantien, then the two energies will be floating around and causing incredible pain to the physical body. It is very possible that over time these massive stray energies can cause significant damage to the physical body and even result in death.

Also, if the student is successful at placing both the yin

chi and yang chi inside of the lower dantien, the duration of time that these two energies can reside in the LDT without causing harm is unclear. For example, if the lower dantien holds yang chi, and yin chi is naturally stored elsewhere, then the yin chi is being held unnaturally in the lower dantien during level four. As such, it is possible that potential consequences could develop over time if the student is not successful in achieving fusion. Also, even if the individual manages to take the yin chi out of the lower dantien, then it will also float around and cause great pain to the body.

During the level four fusion it is also very important to be grounded. If the practitioner is not grounded, the electric qi created could potentially overwhelm the system before being able to become stabilized. If ungrounded, the unnatural level of electric qi generated could theoretically result in human combustion.

Lastly, as many western students have mentioned, if the dantien becomes damaged in this process then it cannot be healed by John Chang. The student will no longer be able to train.

Ultimately, Mo Pai is an interesting technology, but its experimentation brings risk and possible damage to one's body. One can not only achieve similar results, but even better results through following the natural path.

Variance

When compiling perspectives from multiple sources, sometimes disagreements arise between the sources. In such an event it is important to evaluate why each statement was made and the confirmation or reasoning behind it.

Jim McMillan says that meditation is "not necessary for levels 3 and 4," because the practitioner has, "accumulated enough yang to make the dantien full."[16]

AND

Kosta Danaos says, "Level Four is completed strictly by meditation."[17]

When comparing these two statements, the second proves to be more accurate. Looking at past information, it becomes apparent that John Chang took a retreat during this time (level four) to specifically engage in jungle meditation. It would seem the reasoning for Jim McMillan's statement, when saying that meditation is not necessary for level three and four, is rooted in the understanding that no more yang chi needs to be accumulated. As such, Jim McMillan would be strictly viewing meditation as a tool for gathering yang chi, thus creating the assumption that mediation is not necessary. Although meditation is indeed a tool for accumulating chi, meditation can also serve as a means for calming the body/mind and attaining a height of mental silence suitable for activating the LDT in order to facilitate level four fusion.

Super Powers/ Descriptions

Attaining the level four fusion marks a graduation in the Mo Pai lineage. Completing fusion is similar to transforming from a student into a teacher. After the fusion is complete, the student no longer needs a master to continue their training in Mo Pai, and becomes completely self-reliant in regards to future training. At this level they have all the tools necessary to progress without further help.

This achievement is a true step from the ordinary to the extraordinary, and is followed by many super natural phenomena. After achieving level four fusion, besides attaining the electric qi, John Chang realized an arsenal of other new abilities and attainments. Many of these attainments, such as the ability to communicate across the world, seem impossible to the western understanding of the nature of reality.

THE SECOND PATH

Many people who study Mo Pai believe it to be the only path to immortality. A type of special technology serving to unlock the secret to life after death. This is not the correct approach. Looking at the texts, John Chang himself never makes the claim that Mo Pai is the only way to become immortal, and in fact he speaks of a second way.

"My teacher said there are two methods to gain nirvana that allow you to pass from the process of continual reincarnation." [18]

–Jim McMillan

The other path to immortality and nirvana is the natural path or often referred to as "The Way." Mo Pai itself was created as a technology based on knowledge of the natural, conscious evolutionary progression of man towards immortality and nirvana. Immortality and attaining a conscious state of heaven on Earth is not kept behind lock and key.

"The ultimate goal is to realize who you are, to become one with God, to become a god. This is what we call Theosis. We are gods,' Daskalos said, 'but we are not aware of it. We suffer from a self-inflicted amnesia. The aim,' he reiterated many times, 'is to reawaken that which we have always been and we shall always be."

–Daskalos[19]

In actuality, anyone, anywhere, is able to attain conscious immortality and take their yang with them after death regardless of their background or lineage association. In other words, the fusion of yin chi and yang chi is a natural evolutionary occurrence that does not require methods.

"These powers do seep out unexpectedly at very rare times in some people who have never trained."

–Jim McMillan[20]

Supernatural powers awaken in those who achieve the natural form of fusion. These people are typically the ones that ascend in consciousness by way of lifestyle. Many times, they are the ones who are interweaving their work and play to achieve a constant synthesis of living in the moment. These people also may be regularly participating in some form of creating, whether it be the musician, painter, writer, etc.

Creating has a special quality to it that sets the individual out of ordinary replicated belief systems, and into a concentration based mental-state. In the creative process, the creator takes control. Creating can be seen as using awareness to go beyond the mind. John Chang himself has mentioned how yin and yang come together during the process of creation. This may not be the same as attaining Mo Pai fusion, but being a creator certainly is a concentration-based practice.

It is up to each individual to find and consistently practice their method of stillness. What action or tool they can use that will put them in the present moment, creating silence in the midst of the world's chaos and generating a state peace.

"It is difficult to sit still in our day and age, but stillness is the key to success in the end. We are overstimulated by our environment. It is hard to keep your thoughts in the present moment, isn't it? You are always looking ahead, looking back, worried about this, angered by that. You must put your mind on where you are now, not where you were or where you want to be." "I cannot tell you how. Each must find their own way." [21]

–John Chang

John Chang is familiar with the natural ascension process. When John is referring to how each must find their own way, he is talking about finding our own individual technique or method for silence. Creating this stillness is the key for one's concentration to develop. It is an individual's method to become fully present and place the mind where one is now, dissolving all extraneous thoughts. The action that <u>creates silence</u> in the midst of the world's chaos and sets the individual here and now. A form of outward awareness meditation serving to activate the etheric body and allow one to achieve natural fusion.

"The sage chooses action to achieve non-action."

-Lao Tzu

In the quote, Lao Tzu is referring to using action to still the mind. The non-action is of the mind, achieving silence.

Finding this particular action can be anything worth doing, however it is often referred to as finding one's "work" or sole-purpose (soul-purpose). The action or work by an individual that awakens the soul and quiets the mind. For some this can be writing, art, music, cooking, constructing, or anything that creates silence for the individual, everyone is unique. This is commonly simply referred to as following one's heart. But in the modern world, the alchemical importance of following one's heart has been widely disregarded.

Through following one's work/heart and discovering more about one's self, individuals become more sensitive to their experience. They begin learning what actions to take that further enrich the conscious experience. Through doing so, one attains a constant outward meditative state. Constantly participating in this process is what eventually takes a person to the immortal experience.

> *"It is not a question of discovering the "I" but of expressing it. This is the purpose of the Research for Truth, to find out who you are and to express yourself as you ought to."*[22]

> *–Daskalos*

This means that in order to reach the god-self, one needs to not only know who they are, but actually express themselves. For example, one does not figure out that they love singing and then instantly become enlightened. Enlightenment comes from *expressing* oneself as a singer through continual practice. It is the facilitation of a continual awareness-based silence, or in this case, regularly singing as a method of training and refining one's concentration. This is very similar to practicing meditation on a regular basis. Traditionally, finding one's "way" was a natural process, but the common mindset of modern day society has lost touch with the value of conscious ascension and caused many to stray away from self-discovery.

> *The Grandmaster said, "The first requirement for learning the Way is hard work; then you need to learn to be a member of society, which means doing good and refraining from evil, building up character. When you have developed virtue and built up character, eventually you enter naturally into the Way."*
>
> -Wang Liping, *Enter the Dragon Gate*[23]

This process does not have to take decades, or even a decade, but can actually take only a short period of time. The process depends on how much one is willing to invest in themselves.

Doing good and refraining from evil helps one to destroy extraneous thoughts that hinder one from silence. However, the process of conscious evolution is not about one-sided unconditional giving. Many have the view that life is about constantly giving in order to attain heaven in the afterlife. In a certain sense this approach is missing the point; finding one's way is about giving and receiving at the same time. It is about finding what one can do for others, but doing it because it empowers them while they do it. They do not do the work for others, but for the silence associated with doing the work.

In other words, when a person finds "their way", they will know it, because their experience begins to shift, leading one to a deeper realization of the self while they perform the work. This is "soul purpose." Purpose lead by the soul. Because one's purpose in life directly corresponds to activating one's soul and shifting/increasing one's experience, or relationship with reality. Soul-purpose is a continual process of self-realization.

> *Knowing others is intelligence; knowing yourself is true wisdom.*
>
> -Lao Tzu

Alchemists know that true wisdom comes from deepening the conscious experience of life. True wisdom cannot be gained by words or study, but only by the direct participation with reality.

By knowing one's self, one is directly entering into a meditative state. Jim McMillan made the observation that many people are entering into meditative states without realizing it.

> "Some people naturally breathe in a slow rhythmic manner while in a deep

concentrated focus, which is just one common method of chi gong training."

–Jim McMillan[24]

People engage in awareness meditation without realizing it because meditation is a technique developed by observing natural progression. The people are not emulating meditation, it is meditation that is emulating conscious people. That is what makes meditation such a powerful tool for most individuals, because it can help lead them to truth in their outward lives. A consistent practice of meditation can be compared to holding one's hand and walking them towards their soul-purpose.

Alchemical Systems

Throughout history, many ancient philosophers, alchemists, wizards, and priests have studied the natural, evolutionary, conscious progression of man. In doing so, they have carefully created techniques and methods for assisting the process of attaining immortality and nirvana. The techniques created replicate the natural process of ascension and can be related to "hacking" the process in order to achieve results.

These systems are normally based on first building the individual's foundation, and then leading one towards the fusion of yin and yang chi.

Many methods and techniques have been created over time by various sects and masters around the globe to achieve fusion. Commonly people may study methods residing under lineages associated with titles such as Zen Meditation, Taoist Alchemy, Kundalini Yoga, Western Hermetics, and Buddhist Meditation. These systems are utilizing practices to focus on purifying and activating the etheric nervous system of each individual to the highest potential.

In the midst of the dantiens and various energy channels, the single most significant aspect of the path of conscious progression is the opening of the sacred disks (chakras). The chakras are energy points along the spine that increase the power of the nervous system, literally expanding ones relationship with their human body/mind.

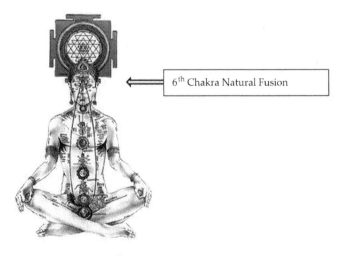

6th Chakra Natural Fusion

Chakra Diagram*   25

In conscious progression, one naturally opens each of the chakras/energy centers in the etheric body from the ground up. Each new chakra brings a higher level of concentration and awareness. The various systems around the world have many different routes and techniques for activating the etheric body, and some even disregard the chakras all together. Nonetheless, the chakras/energy centers are still there in the background, and being affected.

Many are familiar with yoga. Yoga was actually originally called yog. The "a" at the end only came about because British people visited India and then afterwards went around saying yog, but because of their heavy accent people heard "yoga" instead. The true term "yog" in Hindi means *union*. This is because, the true goal of yoga is to create union between the prana and apana energies at the sixth chakra. To create fusion.

When the initiate finally opens the 6th chakra, the yin chi and yang chi come together producing a fusion inside the cranium. At this point the practitioner becomes able to feel and see yin chi. Because of this, the initiate can see spirits and also the second layer energy signatures of others. More importantly, at this point the practitioner becomes able to perform absolute meditation, concentrating beyond the mind

Throughout all of these paths, it is the awareness that is being trained, either indirectly through techniques or directly through meditation practice.

Awareness is both the path and the destination.

–Zen proverb

Many sects disregard the variety of techniques available. They base their understanding in the knowledge that during natural progression one is training the awareness. So these practitioners train the awareness directly through meditation and allow the energy centers to open naturally. This will be explained in more detail with examples.

Power Variance

Jim McMillan's advice on Qi Gong, "When comparing the two systems you'll find that you can illustrate some abilities rather early in chi gong. In contrast, Nai Gong will take longer because rather than advancing up the levels so quickly, Nai Gong develops each level to its max. And thereby has a much greater foundation to build power from at each level."[26]

There is a large power difference between level four Mo Pai and natural fusion; Mo Pai fusion is over hundreds of times more powerful. This is because the fusion in the Mo Pai training occurs in and consists of all the chi available in the lower dantien. Whereas in natural fusion, the chi is fused at the location of the sixth chakra, occurring at a small energy cavity in the brain. John Chang describes his fusion experience as lightening surging through his body. The experience even caused him to faint in his early attempts. In natural fusion, however, the master will just see an extremely bright light.

MO PAI VS NATURAL PROGRESSION

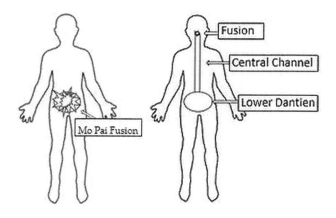

The power difference and the amount of electric qi generated is substantial.

The lower dantien is the foundation for the chi being fused. Some yoga systems teach that the power behind the kundalini comes from the first chakra. This is not correct and is more of a simplification. The true power comes from the lower dantien or also known as the Kanda bulb in more refined forms of yoga. The chi in the lower dantien rises up during concentration meditation and creates more electric qi at the sixth chakra where yin chi and yang chi meet. For this reason, the practitioner who attains natural fusion is not limited in power, and can continue to make electric qi indefinitely. Their power does not hit a ceiling; it is just a much smaller fusion to begin with when compared to Mo Pai. The Mo Pai system has a greater foundation in the sense that a much larger amount of power is generated from the fusion. However, this does not mean a practitioner of natural fusion is unable to achieve the same amount of power in the future with further meditation training.

It is important to understand that the electric qi is not an end-point or "final achievement" in energy cultivation. Later with progress, the electric qi is refined to greater and more subtle forms of energies (golden light). For this reason in many Taoist lineages they teach that it is more efficient to put emphasis on **not expending** the electric qi, so as to utilize it in order to hasten the cultivation of more refined energies required for greater heights of immortality.

The practitioner who achieves normal fusion unlocks two important attainments. The first is conscious immortality during this lifetime, they can take their yang chi with them after death.

The second, is the ability to engage in absolute concentration, this level of practitioner can concentrate one-pointedly beyond the mind. The individual will be able to sit completely present for long periods of time without losing themselves in thought. One-pointed concentration is a powerful training method for gathering chi. As such, the gap in power between Mo Pai fusion and natural fusion may be large initially, but with continual training the gap will gradually fade away.

David Verdesi - Qi Gong Connection

One of the western students that was training in the Mo Pai lineage with John Chang directly, began to develop health problems from the training. This student eventually ended up leaving John Chang's Mo Pai school and went to China in order to find a different energy cultivation system to train under. He was just a beginner when he first started training Mo Pai, but after he left for China he made significant progress. In just a few years later he claimed having achieved fusion of yin chi and yang chi.[27]

The student being described is David Verdesi. Verdesi quit his studies with the Mo Pai lineage and went to study under Qi Gong masters in China. The form of Qi Gong that he encountered cultivates both yin chi and yang chi with a focus on attaining a fusion of the two, similar to Mo Pai. However, the fusion attained at this Qi Gong school is that of natural fusion.

The master who teaches the Qi Gong system that David Verdesi studied is Jiang Feng. Mr. Feng currently uses his chi power to heal people at his prestigious hospital in China. Master Jiang Feng does not use bulls or the energy of any other large animals to transfer powers to his students, as McMillan commonly described in his encounters with qi gong teachers. Actually, Mr. Feng uses techniques and methods to accelerate a person's natural conscious evolution. He has many students that have attained fusion in only a few years of training, and some who have been noted to be able to perform small-scale demonstrations of emitting the "electric qi."

In the last few years, there have surfaced many YouTube videos of Jiang Feng himself demonstrating his ability to emit qi by burning a variety of different objects. Also, there are videos posted of his students performing similar feats, like levitating paper. These feats often involve affecting objects from a distance, which is important because John Chang teaches that one needs both yin chi and yang chi for energy to leave the body.[29]

The focus of this Qi Gong lineage is not for purposes of war, but towards refining one's self and attaining the highest stages of immortality. The powers in this system just come as a result of the process.

> "Individuals who have reached t'ai chi and combined yin and yang inside their beings retain all awareness, memory, and ability after death."[28]

An individual who achieves fusion in their being through either Mo Pai, Qi Gong, or concentration, will take their yang chi with them after death. They will be able to be themselves after death and not be lost. This applies to both the natural path and Mo Pai. The individual who does not attain fusion will not be free. As John Chang has described in *The Magus of Java*, after death these individuals will lose the ability to feel or express themselves truly, and become bounded by previous habits and traits.

Wim Hof

Over the last decade, Wim Hof, also known as the "ice-man," received a lot of global media attention because of his rare ability to personally withstand sub-zero temperatures for long periods of time.

The ability for Hof to withstand cold temperatures has to do with him increasing the potential of his etheric body. Through his continual training in the cold, he became able to silence his mind to such a degree necessary for natural fusion to occur.

By fusing the yin and yang energies inside of his body, Hof has unlocked what some Taoist alchemists refer to as the "thermonuclear engine." This enables Hof to use his internal power to stay warm. Similar to Wim Hof, John Chang and his teacher Liao Che Tung also mention using their internal energy to generate heat, allowing them to remain warm in the midst of freezing cold temperatures.[30] These masters are using the fused form of their internal energy to create heat inside their bodies in order to keep themselves warm.

Through continual interaction with his awareness during his time in nature, Wim Hof was able to build his etheric foundation and create the environment necessary to achieve complete silence of the mind. For Hof, his method focused on developing his awareness through continual interaction with the sensory perception associated with feeling.

The Tibetan Buddhists teach a similar technique involving five different vehicles which are used as tools for placing the awareness on in order to lead one to quieting the mind. The vehicles represent the five senses including touch, taste, olfactory, sound, and vision. By concentrating on one of these senses, the disciple is stepping out of their thought process and practicing one-pointed concentration to still his/her mind.[31]

John Chang teaches that everyone is unique and must find their "way" to silence. For Wim Hof, through continual practice involved with concentrating on his perceptions associated with feeling, he was able to experience the complete mental stillness. This experience of complete silence was the beginning of his career as "ice-man."

"Lose your mind and come to your senses."

– Fritz Perls

Telling his story, Wim Hof reflects on a life changing experience that began his career as iceman. It all started one day when he was at a lake. He had a certain calling to immerse himself in the cold water. Wim Hof says, "When I got into the water, I really felt a mighty feeling coming over me, after 30 seconds I felt great. *Then I think that is one of my first moments where my mind got still.* No side effects anymore, no thoughts anymore, just feeling."[32]

It is no coincidence that Wim Hof directly relates his grand experience to that of silencing the mind. Just like John Chang in the jungle, at this height of complete stillness Wim

Hof became a master and merged the yin chi and yang chi in his body. This is the same experience that John Chang is referring to when he exemplifies the extreme importance of reaching total stillness and silence (natural fusion). Or finding one's way to silence. After Wim Hof's profound experience of complete mental silence while inside the lake, his life changed forever, and so began the "Ice Man's" career.

> "Right now I am focused from within, so I feel strong and warm. Power is inside like an energy."[32]

> –Wim Hof

Wim Hof continually uses meditation techniques to refine and increase his power. In the videos he explains how he is often practicing meditation for hours at a time in a freezer, and he also even hints at chakras being the source of his power.[32] As his power has been increasing through his training, he has been performing many feats around the world. On one occasion he ran half a marathon in the Arctic Circle. Other performances include him climbing the slopes of Mt. Everest to an altitude of twenty-two thousand feet only wearing shorts. Also sitting motionless with direct contact with ice one hour and twelve minutes. These miraculous and seemingly unexplainable feats that he has performed around the world gained him a total of thirteen world records.

In the video, a medical professional from the Harvard

Institute says that he believes it is possible to use these altered states to perhaps prevent disease. However, using altered states to achieve beneficial results for the body is not cutting edge or even new information. Sages have known and practiced techniques for developing the highest potential of the human body for centuries all around the world. These masters have known that the cultivation of higher energies will heal disease and increase the potency of the immune system, and more. It would seem science is slowly accepting the reality of human potential. The iceman is just the tip of the iceberg.

Post-Fusion

LEVELS 5-72

"Mo Pai's ultimate and final goal is the same as several of the other Asian religions that also seek nirvana. This clearly illustrates there is a connection between all these different religion systems and chi development."

–Jim McMillan[1]

After completing level four fusion, the practitioner continues to train with the determination to eventually reach level seventy-two. Reaching level seventy-two in Mo Pai is referred to by John Chang as attaining a form of ultimate nirvana. The level seventy-two achievement is similar to beating the final boss in a video game, except in this case, the game has to do with a person's entire existence. The training at this point is shrouded in mystery, however John Chang has presented a few clues as to what the post-fusion training is about.

Near the end of Liao Che Tung's (John Chang's Sifu) life, John Chang was given an ancient book to help guide his training to level seventy-two. Most of the details and contents of the ancient book of seventy-two levels are unknown to the west. However, dialogs between John Chang and his western students, and also the accounts of great masters in the past, reveal primary characteristics regarding the seventy-two levels of Mo Pai.

There are two significant aspects regarding the Mo Pai book of seventy-two levels. The first characteristic is that the levels serve as a measuring stick based on an individual's power. In other words, the Mo Pai system of seventy-two levels serves as a form of measuring stick that is placed up to a master and used to measure their current power and their power rating is what determines their current level. The second primary aspect, is that the method for attaining power is universal and is not confined to the Mo Pai lineage.

Level Measuring

When referring to the difference in levels, John Chang simply says: "The power doubles."[2]

After the level four fusion is attained, a master's current "level" is determined based on the amount of power that they have attained. After fusion, a master progresses by one level every time his/her power doubles. This means that level five has twice the power of level four, and level six has twice the power of level five. This introduces the idea of a system based on structured progression.

The legendary training manual serves as a *measuring*

stick for practitioners as they continue to train. By judging one's power level they can see how far they have progressed. There are a variety of different power tests for the practitioner to endeavor to accomplish in order to progress past each level.

> "It is important to understand that all true masters do not consider superpowers as their final objective. Rather, superhuman abilities to them are only a way to judge their path to alleged nirvana."

> –Jim McMillan[3]

Powering Up

Once fusion has been attained, the ultimate method of accumulating chi is for the practitioner to engage in absolute meditation. It is not in using the mind or techniques, but in transcending the mind, and entering intense states of concentration that large amounts of chi can be gathered.

Before fusion, absolute meditation is not available to the practitioner. Attaining fusion actually shifts the practitioner's concentration to an entirely new level. They gain the ability to concentrate beyond the mind and enter into absolute meditation at any time they wish.

Accomplishing mastery of the mind leads one towards mastery of the physical body. With further training, this eventually allows practitioners like John Chang to sustain absolute concentration for long periods of time. Meditations can last days, weeks, or even months. During these meditations the breath of the master is reduced to the breathless state and the physical body is left in a state of suspended animation. The body sustains itself in this state by naturally performing khechari mudra and receiving continual sustenance.

Looking at the past, a majority of the greatest masters in human history did not actually train Mo Pai. However, all of them have been recorded training absolute meditation for long periods of time: days, weeks, months, and some even years. Attaining mastery of the mind and sustaining extraordinary lengths of absolute concentration is what creates true masters. If a master is able to attain fusion through one of the many routes, they will then have the necessary foundation to progress towards level 72 without the need of further instruction.

Through his consistent training, John Chang has achieved a degree of awareness and power to be considered in league with the greatest masters in the world. Just by closing his eyes he is able to sense other masters around the globe and their level of attainment. John Chang says there are at least ten other masters alive today who share a power level at a similar degree or above his own.[4] John Chang emphasizes that some of these masters are *much more* powerful than himself.

Two of the greatest masters in the last two thousand years are Damo (Bhodidharma) and Chang San Geng. Both of these masters, as stated by John Chang, were able to reach level 72 (the highest possible level) in Mo Pai during their human existence on Earth.[5]

BHODIDHARMA

The great Bhodidharma, born around 470 AD, was able to reach the infamous level seventy-two during his human lifetime. Bhodidharma is important to mention because he, however, is not noted to have trained Mo Pai. His training methods are actually similar to those transmitted by Buddha in the Lankavatara Sutra. Throughout his life, Bhodidharma had many disciples and spent a great amount of time in temples (notably Shaolin), spreading his direct teachings and allowing them to be recorded and preserved. Bhodidharma is an important clue because he helps illustrate how the levels beyond fusion in Mo Pai are actually a form measuring system used for judging the extent of one's development. In this context, the extent of one's supernatural prowess is directly connected to the extent of their conscious relationship with the universe.

Bhodidharma's training does not actually consist of any "secret" techniques, but instead a form of "true" understanding. He teaches that the ultimate technique is sustaining conscious awareness beyond the mind. He teaches that the source of all techniques comes from the same place. So by training one's awareness they are transcending all possible techniques. This is where Bhodidharma's training is rooted. He teaches that his technique surpasses all techniques, because in all techniques one is directing their awareness to their mind to perform a technique. So when purely training the awareness (real mind), one surpasses any technique that could be formulated by the mind.

There exist recorded discussions between himself and disciples that convey his teachings.

> Bodhidharma's disciple Eka asked, "If someone is committed to seeking the Buddha's Way, what methods for training should he give heed to?"
>
> Bodhidharma replied, "Since meditation embraces all methods and practices, I call it the essential one."
>
> Eka asked, "How can one single method embrace all practices?"
>
> Bodhidharma replied, "It is the root and source of all methods, all methods are simply products of the mind so, if you are able to thoroughly comprehend what 'real mind' is, then your myriad practices will be fully equipped.
>
> Your 'real mind' is a great tree; its branches, blossoms and fruit all depend completely on the root, even a severed tree will survive if its root is intact whereas a fully grown tree, once detached from its root will die. If you train in the Way with a thorough comprehension of what 'real mind' is, then you will conserve your strength as you easily succeed in

> realizing Buddhahood but, if you train without thoroughly comprehending what 'real mind' is, then you will squander your efforts to no avail."[6]

This form of training is using awareness to lead one to conscious immortality. By being in awareness and letting go of stray thoughts, the practitioner is developing the etheric body. With this method, one is ascending the chakras and eventually attaining natural fusion. Then after fusion, engaging in absolute meditation to gain further power.

Being one of the greatest masters in human history, Bhodidharma is famous for his long meditations. At one point it is even believed that he entered suspended animation for a total of nine years near the Shoalin Monastery in northern China.[7]

Mr. Lim – Renegade Master

This master is mentioned several times in *The Magus of Java*, but his training methods remain a mystery. What is apparent is that he was able to attain a high level in a very short time span.

The story goes that Mr. Lim was an evil tax collecting warlord who was crippled and turned into a beggar at the feet of Pai Lok Nen (Liao's sifu). In retribution for his crimes, Pai Lok Nen spared Lim's life, but ripped out his eye balls using a kung fu technique. Later on, Pai Lok Nen reflects on this first encounter with Mr. Lim when they fought and Nen ripped his eyes out, and makes an interesting comment. Nen mentions that *Mr. Lim was already at a somewhat high level when they first fought.*[8] This is interesting, because at this time Mr. Lim was a warlord and had no association with the Mo Pai lineage and yet he was still regarded as being at a somewhat high level. Another interesting aspect is that Pai Lok Nen is judging Lim, who at the time has no association with the Mo Pai, as if using the Mo Pai level system to evaluate a specimen. It can be compared to using the scouter in *Dragon Ball Z*. These small circumstances simply give insight into the "universal power level" gauging system of the Mo Pai seventy-two levels.

Following the first battle and losing his eyes to Pai Lok Nen, Lim wanted more power and obviously could not turn to the Mo Pai system. So instead, Lim found and trained under a different school that is apparently just as ancient and powerful. Mr. Lim only trained for a total of ten years and accumulated enough power to be considered in the level 50s. At this level of power, he became a skilled opponent for even Pai Lok Nen. Mr. Lim began this training in his 70s and then died in his 80s during his second battle with Pai Lok Nen.[9]

The significance of this master holds two important aspects. One is that the appearance of this master at a high level of attainment shows that the legendary Mo Pai book of 72 levels is not required for higher level training. Also equally important, is that this master demonstrates that it is possible to reach high levels (in the 50s) in just a very short period of time.

WANG LIPING

"I am specifically talking about one very high level teacher in China today…"

> "I know that this Chinese master is highly developed in some abilities Pak John isn't capable of doing."
>
> –Jim McMillan[10]

The secret master often being referred to in Jim McMillan's texts is Wang Liping. Wang Liping has become very popular over the past ten years following the surface and circulation of his biography *Enter the Dragon Gate* in the west. Wang Liping currently has two books, both of them explaining his training methods and achievements. The books mentioned are *Enter the Dragon Gate* and *Ling Bao Tong Zhi Neng Nei Gong Shu*.

Jim McMillan has also claimed that Wang Liping is a level thirty-five master.[11] However, the circumstances regarding how Jim McMillan arrived at this information is unclear. However, level thirty-five is not unreasonable considering the training and attainments in Liping's biography.

Reading his official bibliography, it becomes apparent that Wang Liping has gone through very extensive training his whole life. He has personally lived the teenage life that every martial artist dreams of. Wang Liping's authorized bibliography tells of him possessing many abilities similar to John Chang, like that of levitation, shooting chi blasts, and also a few more unknown to the Mo Pai texts, like invisibility and the yang shen double.[12]

Over the years, Wang Liping has personally taught many classes to numerous students around the world. His inner alchemy system, sometimes referred to as the "The Dragon Gate" lineage, teaches many longevity practices, or "equilibrium practices," that balance the energies of the body in relation to the cosmos. Techniques of this nature are efficient for achieving longevity and healing disease. Primarily, however, his technique for self-cultivation is full-lotus meditation with emphasis on cultivating awareness beyond the mind. This practice is *very* similar to Bhodidharma's technique, but seems to be explained a little differently by Wang Liping's teachers.

In his training, Wang Liping is told by his teacher to sit in full-lotus posture and to clear random thoughts and enter stillness. When Wang Liping had trouble with this, his masters would tell him their method for achieving stillness of the mind:

> "To clear away random thoughts," he began in reply, "first use formal judgment to deal with them. As soon as a random thought arises, immediately pass judgment on it: either declare it right, or declare it wrong, or declare that this is as far as it goes. Having made this determination, stop right away and do not allow rumination to go on and on.

Then random thoughts will vanish by
themselves, and in this way you can enter
into stillness."[13]

This is a technique for increasing conscious awareness
and naturally opening the energy centers/chakras along the
spine, until finally achieving fusion. There is a large similarity
between Wang Liping's technique and Bhodidharma's
technique. These techniques are using awareness meditation
with the idea of resting in the original mind and not allowing
the "stained mind" to fog one's awareness. When asked by his
disciples what the most important aspects of his training were,
Wang Liping would teach his students to first focus on stilling
the mind (attaining fusion) and then practice concentration
(absolute meditation).

This framework is telling students to create stillness in
the mind until attaining fusion, and then engage in absolute
meditation. Absolute meditation is the key to the higher levels.
As mentioned earlier, as one deepens their concentration in
meditation their breath also slows down. The breath eventually
slows down to a complete stop at higher levels of concentration.

After one year of training "quieting the mind
meditation" for four hours per day Wang Liping experienced
what many would refer to as a fusion. Shortly after attaining
fusion, Wang Liping held the breathless state for over twenty-
eight days when he was still in his teens training in the
mountains with his masters.[14]

Wang Liping has not displayed any abilities on film,

possibly because he does not want to attract the wrong form of attention. However one thing is for sure, and that is that Liping has gathered a lot of respect from the cultivation community around the globe. Over the years, there have also surfaced many reports of him performing extraordinary acts, even to the extent of manipulating the weather for his government on special occasions.[15] I urge all people with interest in inner alchemy to read the texts available surrounding Wang Liping.

The Secret of the Golden Flower

Chapter Two, Part Nine

The method used by the ancients for escaping from the world consisted in refining away the dregs of yin in order to return to the pure Qian. It is just a matter of dissolving the lower self (earthly po-soul) and completing the higher self (celestial hun-soul). Turning the light around is the method of dissolving yin and controlling the lower self. Except for the secret of turning the light around, there is no other exercise to return to Qian. **The light itself is Qian; to turn it around is to return to it. Just persist in this method, and naturally vitality-water will be sufficient,** spirit-fire will ignite, intent-earth will stabilize and **thus the holy embryo gestates.**[16]

PROGRESSION

After fusion has occurred the practitioner will become an immortal, and they will retain their yang chi after death. The idea of immortality is that the yin-yang fusion attained by the practitioner *never goes away*, not even after the death of the physical body. Considering the fusion of the energies is permanent, and lasts even after death, it is fair to say that the Mo Pai master no longer needs to go through levels one through four again in order to create additional amounts of electric qi. The master at this level will automatically create the electric qi they need from the yin and yang chi they absorb. Meaning, from this point forward, the master needs only to proceed to **accumulate** more yin and yang chi through absolute meditation. Absolute meditation for long periods of time is the most powerful form of gathering yin chi and yang chi. During a period of intense training, John Chang, for example, left his home for two years and lived in the mountains sustaining himself off of roots and plants in an isolated cave while constantly practicing meditation.[17]

Mastering the mind and gaining the ability to engage in absolute concentration results in a new plateau in the capability to accumulate chi. Looking at the texts, it takes eighty hours of absolute meditation in order to fill the lower dantien and complete level one. For new students, accomplishing this feat can sometimes take up to five to ten years. The reason level one takes so long is because the accumulation of chi is hindered by the practitioner's lack of absolute concentration. Now when considering how quickly a post-fusion master can gather the amount of yang chi required for level one, the time frame changes dramatically. John Chang for example, can enter into an awareness beyond the mind and step into the "breathless state," engaging in absolute meditation for over a week without stopping. This allows him to attain his eighty hours of absolute concentration multiple times, gathering enough energy to fill his LDT not once, but twice in a little over a week. John Chang, through absolute meditation, accumulates in just a few days the amount of chi that it takes most people five years of consistent training. In this model, the student takes five years (1,825 days) to complete level one and the master can complete level one in eighty hours (3.3 days). This shows that engaging in absolute meditation is over 550 times more potent at gathering chi than a normal human's meditation practice.[18]

As a potent means to gain chi, absolute meditation also becomes an important tool for gaining and enhancing superhuman abilities. Those who have attained fusion through natural means will have difficulty attaining these abilities without meditation (absolute concentration for long periods of time).

> Student: "There is that much difference in power? Between level 40 and 50?"
>
> John Chang: "Yes, same with level 20 and 30 and 30 and 40."[19]

Considering there is the same difference in power between level twenty and thirty, thirty and forty, and forty and fifty, it introduces the idea of structured progression in the Mo

Pai system based on measuring power levels.

Climbing the ladder, the road becomes steeper as the practitioner goes up in level because each level after four (referred to as level three in the Indonesian system) requires twice the amount of power as the previous. Therefore, the task of reaching a higher level becomes more difficult as one progresses in level. This means that the masters actually slow down as they go higher, and have more difficulty when passing the higher levels.

The steep slope can be observed when looking at Liao Che Tung's history. Tung first started training with Pai Lok Nen as a level one student when he was around thirty-five years old. By the age of forty he attained level twenty-six and by the age of forty-five he had progressed to around level thirty.[20] If we consider that it took Liao Che Tung around one year to reach level four, this means it took him around four years in order to reach level twenty-six. This shows he progressed twenty-two levels in only an estimated four years of training after achieving fusion. However, in the next five years of isolated training, he only progressed another five to seven levels. The higher levels became much more difficult. This example displays how quickly the lower levels are accomplished in relation to the higher levels. Liao Che Tung's progress had been cut by a little over three times.

John Chang says that the, "<u>task</u> grows more difficult," and not easier, after each level.[21]

As the power requirement for each level becomes more immense, this causes the timeframe to completion to expand, or in other words, the task to grow.

Looking at chi accumulation from the perspective of absolute meditation, a master at level four will have an amount of yang chi estimated at 160 hours of absolute meditation. This is because a level two student should have twice the yang chi as a level one student, and also because levels three and four do not accumulate yang chi.[22] (Levels three and four are primarily concerned with manipulating and fusing the chi). In order to double in power after the level four fusion and complete level five, it takes the master another 160 hours of absolute meditation. Following this logic, it also means that it takes 320 hours of absolute meditation to complete level six. Considering that each level requires the practitioner to accumulate twice the amount of chi compared to the previous level, the training requirements quickly increase dramatically. A practitioner may be able to complete level five within a week of straight meditation after completing level four, however level six will take twice that amount of time, and level seven twice of that. Because the increasing power requirements are on an exponential scale, the later levels can take the practitioner an entire year of intensive training just to complete.[23]

Level	Hours of Absolute Concentration
5	160
6	320
7	640

Looking at the absolute meditation requirements for the first few levels depicts how Liao Che Tung was able to complete twenty-two levels after experiencing fusion in only an estimated four years of training.

However, this type of analysis quickly becomes ineffective. One has to be careful when graphing meditation progression for long periods of time, because it is not a two-dimensional process. A powerful factor that is being disregarded at this point is that the power, or intensity, of the meditation also increases with practice. In other words, the master's concentration increases as they train, which in effect increases the actual potency of the absolute meditation's ability to gather chi. A great master like John Chang may use up a lot of his power through his routine healings, but he has an intensity of concentration available which allows him to accumulate the large amounts of energy back in a reasonable time frame. Liao Che Tung was also credited with often displaying intense concentration through superhuman levels of speed and reaction. One example is when he took a piece of paper from his friend's desk so fast it seemed he was pulling it out of his pocket.[24]

TAOIST ALCHEMY

Similar to the Mo Pai's system of seventy-two levels, ancient Toaist alchemists also developed a different system of rankings and graduations to gauge one's attainment. The information and levels of achievement in cultivation from other

Taoist lineages can be compared with Mo Pai to give insight into some of the unanswered questions. Common Taoist alchemy has five primary levels of attainment: ghost immortal, human immortal, earth immortal, spiritual immortal, and celestial immortal.

There are also two primary classifications of chi in Taoist Alchemy. There is Post-Celestial (Xian Tian) chi and Pre-Celestial (Hou Tian) chi.

Post-Celestial

Post-celestial chi comes from the earth (yin chi) and the air (yang chi) that we breathe. Post-celestial chi is the form of chi that is utilized and developed in the Mo Pai system. Through the first four levels, the Mo Pai practitioner gathers and fuses the post-celestial yin chi, gathered from the earth, and the post-celestial yang chi, gathered from the air. The fusion of these two energies creates the electric qi that John Chang uses to heal his patients through acupuncture needles.

At level four in Mo Pai, the initiate fuses post-celestial yin chi and post-celestial yang chi in the lower dantien to become immortal. In Daoist alchemy, after one has attained fusion of the post-celestial chi they become what is known as an "earth immortal." According to Daoist alchemy this type of immortal survives after the death of the physical body on earth, but they must still rely on and continue to replenish post-celestial chi to exist. Earth immortals remain in the world forever.[25] When the earth eventually goes away, an Earth

Immortal will no longer have a source of which to gather energy in order to survive. Thus, it is proposed, from a Taoist alchemical perspective, that a level four Mo Pai master may live as long as the Earth itself, but they are not truly free from the cycle of death and rebirth. They will still eventually perish. Similarly, when asked, John Chang explains how he regards a level four practitioner as an immortal, but not a true Hsien.[26]

Besides the coinciding phenomenon of electric qi, from the standpoint of Daoist alchemy it would make sense why a level four Mo Pai master is an immortal, but not a true Hsien. A true immortal (Hsien) would be free from the continual chain of death and rebirth.

Pre-Celestial

According to Taoist Alchemy, in order to finally escape the continual cycle of death and rebirth one has to fuse pre-celestial chi. The fusion of pre-celestial chi in Taoist alchemy is known as becoming a spiritual immortal. In other traditions this feat is commonly referred to as enlightenment, becoming an arhat, or simply referred to as completing "The Great Work."

Pre-celestial chi comes from the source; it is beyond this world and its creation. Furthermore, humans only have a finite amount of pre-celestial chi given to them at birth, and when this chi runs out, the body ceases to function. It is said that each one of us is estimated to have enough pre-celestial chi at birth to live 500 years.[27] However, most of the greatest masters, including Bhodidharma, usually do not live past 200.

The process used to greatly increase the longevity of the physical body is to constantly replenish post-celestial chi so that inherent pre-celestial chi goes away at a slower pace.

The fusion of pre-celestial energies does not create the electric qi like the previous fusion, but instead creates an entirely new form of energy often referred to as the *golden light*. This is the golden light that Jesus and many other ascended masters in the past are attributed with using to heal people. More importantly, when pre-celestial chi is fused together one forms what is known as the "light body" or "dharma body." Embodying this form is commonly referred to as enlightenment by many traditions. The "body of light" does not rely on energies from Earth to survive, but instead absorbs energy directly from the Source of Tao, which is beyond this world and its creation. Masters at this level are said to be truly liberated from the continuous cycle of death and rebirth. After death, these masters follow a trail of light out of continual rebirth.[28]

Mo Pai - Level 30

In Mo Pai, there is a large mystery surrounding level thirty. Level thirty is considered a "distinct graduation" where one becomes an hsien, a.k.a. a true immortal.[29] This is like attaining a higher class of being that separates one from those of a lower level. Because of this, it is apparent that something occurs at level thirty that is beyond the normal power level doubling process in the previous levels.

When looking at the Mo Pai level thirty achievement,

there exist distinct similarities with the Taoist pre-celestial fusion. If we look at Liao Che Tung in particular, who is a master that has passed level thirty, he shows distinct differences in ability when compared with John Chang (estimated level twenty-two) who has not passed level thirty.

One of the largest clues that separates Liao Che Tung from John Chang, is Laio's ability to use the *golden wave energy*.

The product from the fusion of post-celestial chi (houtian chi) is like electric power, whereas the product from the fusion of pre-celestial chi (xiantian chi) is like nuclear power.[30] Instead of the electric qi created in the fusion of post-celestial chi, the fusion of pre-celestial chi gives a master control over a new type of energy. This energy is often referred to as the "golden light." From the texts, the golden light energy holds similarities with Mo Pai. Specifically, John Chang would often describe his Sifu's (Liao Che Tung) miraculous ability to use the "golden heat" to cure people of cancer.[31]

The golden heat is a characteristic of a true spiritual immortal. Looking at the texts, John makes it clear that he is not able to create the golden heat like his sifu Liao Che Tung. Liao is above level thirty and John Chang is not. Liao is considered a true immortal in the Mo Pai tradition, and likewise the Taoist alchemists consider one who has fused pre-celestial chi to be a true immortal.

Spiritual immortals (pre-celestial fusion) in Taoist alchemy are also attributed with another mystical ability. This is the ability to consciously be present at several different locations simultaneously. The idea is that their consciousness splits into several different bodies that can perform spiritual work at several different locations simultaneously.[32]

As one develops after becoming enlightened, their superconscious awareness continues to expand to multiple locations at the same time. The individual's consciousness can be simultaneously at seven or more different places, and be able to get impressions and experiences from these locations.[33] The spiritual immortal attribute of being aware of multiple locations simultaneously is also mentioned in the Mo Pai texts. John Chang describes his teacher:

> "Liao Sifu was like a god to me. Since he knew everything I did."[34]

It makes sense how an aspect of John Chang's continuous daily training was actually fueled and motivated by his teacher. More importantly, however, it shows that Liao Sifu was able to be conscious at multiple locations simultaneously. Liao Che Tung, a Mo Pai practitioner above level thirty, had the conscious attribute of an advanced Taoist spiritual immortal.

Note: It is clear that John Chang has the ability to enter into deep meditation and leave his body and become present anywhere on the planet. However, it is not clear if John Chang is also able to be simultaneously aware at several different locations on the planet at the same time.

Going Further

While many of the Mo Pai abilities, attainments, and descriptions connect with the Taoist Spiritual Immortal, there is still a major problem with this theory: John Chang can enter into the breathless state. In the breathless state the physical body enters into suspended animation for long periods of time. John Chang has the ability to meditate for multiple days without stopping.[35] A fusion attained earth immortal can do absolute meditation, concentrating beyond the mind and gaining large amounts of chi at a fast pace. Yet, they cannot completely enter into the breathless state. In the breathless state John Chang is able to leave his body.

Another factor is that on many occasions John Chang's students mention his "interesting nature," and how people are instinctively drawn to him.[36] This may not seem like a major factor, but expression of true nature is a major achievement in alchemy. This is the attribute of a spiritual immortal. At the earth immortal stage, the fusion of yin chi and yang chi, the consciousness does not shift into the true self, also known as merging with the primordial self. A being of earth immortal status would not embody an "interesting nature." This level conscious shift only occurs at the level of spiritual immortal.

Because of these two reasons it is safe to say that John Chang is already at the Xian Tian (Spiritual Immortal) level. Looking at John Chang's progression, there is a gap of five years between when he achieved fusion and when he became able to enter the breathless state and leave his body at will. This gap serves as his period of growth from an earth immortal into a spiritual immortal. The technique for progressing from an earth immortal to a spiritual immortal is simply absolute concentration meditation. John Chang achieved lower dantien earth immortal fusion (age thirty-two) and then through further meditation achieved the spiritual immortal level (age ~thirty-seven).

Similarly, in Kriya Yoga, they only teach students to open the first six chakras (earth immortal fusion), because after that one only needs to meditate to progress further. At this point meditation becomes like watching a television screen and viewing various shapes and images.

"In stillness there is movement."

–Lao Tzu

John Chang showing characteristics of the spiritual immortal proves that a level thirty Mo Pai master is more advanced than attaining pre-celestial fusion. However, this does not release the connection in abilities between the Taoist spiritual immortal and the level thirty Mo Pai master. This is because in Taoist Alchemy, a spiritual immortal is not the highest achievement. There is an enormous gap between a spiritual immortal and a celestial immortal for the different abilities to manifest. A spiritual immortal does not gain the ability of golden light or super conscious awareness of multiple locations immediately, these abilities come with further development. A spiritual immortal is very far away from the next plateau of the celestial immortal status in Taoist Alchemy, meaning there is a lot of training in-between. It is said that after becoming a spiritual immortal, it takes around ten years of absolute meditation to reach the level of celestial immortal.

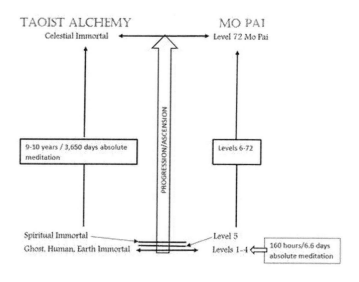

The large gap between a spiritual immortal is very similar to the gap between a level four Mo Pai and a level seventy-two Mo Pai. When considering that the Mo Pai levels double in power, John Chang who is level twenty-two is actually not even a third of the way to level seventy-two. Because the power doubles at each level, he is actually closer to 1/15th of the way to level seventy-two. The mountain slope becomes steeper as one travels upward. Liao Che Tung's progression is a good example of this. Considering this, level twenty-two John Chang when compared with Taoist alchemy would not be classified as a very high level spiritual immortal, which makes sense that his abilities are not as developed as his master, e.g. golden light, multiple body awareness.

Karma

Many masters describe karma as being the law of cause and effect, action and reaction. In Taoist alchemy, the master at the spiritual immortal stage of attainment is free from the cycle of death and rebirth, but they are not, however, free from karma.[37] They still have to atone for their actions and must continue to practice.

A level 30+ master in Mo Pai is also not free from karma, the texts show this because in response to his murderous past, John Chang's teacher, Liao Sifu, decided to live the monastic life and devote himself to penitence. The purpose behind this lifestyle is so that after death Liao could devote his powers towards helping other beings in the idea that when he reached the "Lord God", he would be treated mercifully.[38]

Celestial Immortal

The ultimate stage of conscious evolution a person can attain while in human form on Earth in Taoist alchemy is that of the celestial immortal. Attaining the level of spiritual immortal is like peanuts compared to the task of attaining the status of celestial immortal. As mentioned earlier, the spiritual immortal master has to spend nearly a decade of his/her time in motionless absolute concentration in order to reach the ranking of celestial immortal.

The idea behind the spiritual immortal level is that the master forms the "body of light." This body of light still needs to be developed. The master still needs to *merge* with the light. At the celestial immortal level, the master has achieved complete integration of the physical body with the light of the spirit.[39] It is commonly believed that when a master at this level passes away, they can dematerialize and rematerialize anywhere at will.

Masters at this level are still limited to a human life span, but after death, the body vanishes and nothing remains. Similar to George Lucas's *Star Wars* when Darth Vader struck down Obe-Wan Kenobi on the Death Star and he vanished leaving nothing remaining of his body.

When looking at Mo Pai, John Chang says only two masters in all of Chinese history have reached level seventy-two; Bhodidharma and Chang San Geng. It has also been said that when the grave of Bhodidharma was opened, only his shoe remained.

Going Further

The Lower Dantien Rupture

Besides death, the most calamitous injury a practitioner can have the misfortune of confronting during his/her Mo Pai training is the LDT rupture. This injury occurs to students who have been training on a consistent basis and have at least developed the sensation of heat in the lower dantien. When a student at this level haphazardly trains, after breaking the 72-hour rule, the lower dantien becomes at risk of literally exploding and throwing the practitioner into a world of suffering and decline.

The dantien rupture is caused by the interaction between the major energy centers and the lower dantien. This injury can occur to students who have been training the level two practice or further, and even to students who have recently finished level one and barely scratched the surface of the level two practices.

When the practitioner engages in the Mo Pai meditation training, they are either focusing on the lower dantien, the breath, clearing the mind, or concentrating in awareness. By engaging in one of these forms of awareness-based methods, the student is "powering up" and activating the major energy centers. The lower energy centers, specifically the second chakra (Svadhisthana), coincides with the lower dantien. Many will say that the second chakra itself is the lower dantien, but this is not the case. It is misleading because often times the second chakra is associated with a sea of sexual energy, very similar to the lower dantien (jing). The lower dantien and the second chakra are two separate but connected parts of the same system.

When the activation of the lower energy centers occurs, it interacts with the lower dantien causing the yang chi to move rapidly. This interaction between the two, resulting in the *activation of the LDT*, is part of the natural refinement process in Taoist alchemy that refines jing into chi. However, in Mo Pai, this process also brings significant hazard.

If the practitioner has recently had an orgasm, and expelled semen, the lower dantien becomes closed off. The "gates" of the lower dantien close, becoming inaccessible to further yang chi accumulation.[1]

After completing level one the lower dantien is %100 full. When the practitioner steps into level two training, the lower dantien is now compacting the yang chi already stored there from the level one practices and further introducing more yang chi through meditation training. Now, the level two practitioner meets someone they like (hopefully) and has intercourse. This causes the practitioner's overfilled dantien to become closed off and sealed. Next, this student decides to break the golden rule and not wait the seventy-two hours before beginning training. Now, the lower dantien is over one-hundred percent full AND the gates are closed. So at this point when they engage in concentration meditation, this causes the overfilled dantien to *become activated*, resulting in the yang chi inside to begin moving rapidly. With the yang chi moving rapidly inside of the overfilled **sealed container** made of tissue (lower dantien), the movement of chi causes expansion and the lower dantien to literally detonate, similar to a balloon popping. The lower dantien in some cases becomes torn in over four different locations.

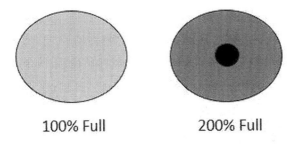

100% Full   200% Full

The dantien rupture injury is completely painless as it occurs on the etheric body and has no initial effects to the physical body. This practitioner will initially just feel a leaking sensation as they begin to leak yang chi (jing in Taoist alchemy) from the lower dantien. The leaking yang jing is warm and thick. Being the least refined, yang jing is the thickest and most distinguishable of the three types of vital energy in Taoist alchemy (jing, chi, and shen). So after the injury, the student will feel the yang jing flowing down the legs constantly, continually, and never stopping. Most of the yang jing leaks in an uneven pattern down the legs and some of the energy becomes stagnant in the stomach area, over time forming large blockages. The blockages over time cause pain and problems to the lower organs (stomach, liver, kidneys).

This injury is not as rare as explained in *The Magus of Java*, it actually occurs occasionally with students who practice chi kung, as they also subject the dantien to dangerous levels of capacity by using compacting methods similar to level two. They place themselves at risk by condensing the jing in the LDT.

> "Training can be very dangerous if done improperly. This has played out with certain westerners. "
>
> –Jim McMillan[2]

A number of westerners (at least three) have claimed to have experienced this injury and sought help from qi gong healers like Jiang Feng. Apparently some have even tried to go directly to John Chang. A few of John Chang's Indonesian students reported these westerners trying make contact with John Chang after the injury, but Chang did nothing for them.[3]

Healing

After rupturing the lower dantien, the student should do everything in their power to find a master capable of healing this injury. If the master requires the student to go to them and they cannot at least leave their body and check on the situation from a distance, well personally I believe one should not waste time with them. The student with this injury needs to find someone competent. Look for the real masters, some of them have even been mentioned in this book. A person can sustain this injury for a while, at least two months, but they need to be doing all that they can to find someone skilled.

The dantien injury heals the same way as a normal injury, however due to the seriousness, it often takes an experienced practitioner to assist. A master healer in some cases can heal this injury in as little as two weeks' time. The master assists by closing the wound and also by redirecting the energy that is flowing out of the dantien so that it does not cause blockages in the stomach and legs. The energy that is leaking is redirected into the meridians in order to keep it in circulation and not create more blockages. Therefore, this requires an experienced teacher, with a decent level of awareness. Think of the energy channels (meridians) like flowing rivers. The leaking energy can be routed into a major meridian, or "river", so as to keep the leaking energy circulating and not dispersing into the legs or stomach and stagnating. Dispersion can eventually cause blockages to form that will affect the nervous system and create numbing sensations, inflammation, and pain.

The capacity for this injury to heal is unique for each person. If one has other forms of disease it will become difficult to heal completely. However, people who have no prior forms of disease, and who will be much less likely to get the injury in the first place, will be much more likely to heal completely. Those who have trouble healing, should use the prescribed methods, but also should focus on perfecting their lifestyle and fixing their faults so as to keep their energy raised and moving towards awakening. An awakened being will naturally heal all forms of disease, because they have no dis-ease (this is connected with the knowledge of Reiki, as will be discussed). Soul-purpose will keep one always in a state of raised kundalini. For the people that do not heal it is a tough spot, but they can still overcome this disease by following the light. This is the idea that Lao Tzu speaks of when giving disease to one's disease.

Technique

For someone who has this injury they should treat it by sleeping with the hands placed over the naval (aka belly button). The naval acts as an energetic hole where excess energy can be vacuumed out of the stomach and into the arms to be recirculated. *(I have a personal theory that the umbilical cord actually sends vital energy directly from the mother into the infant's lower dantien during development.)* The hands are stacked right hand over left hand and then both are placed on top of the naval. The major chakra in each hand creates a sucking and vacuuming effect. The left hand is the energetic receiving hand, while the right hand is the giving. By placing the right over left, the right hand serves as an amplifier for the left hand to increase the vacuuming effect. The stagnant chi and blockages that have formed from leaking will be sucked into the hands through the naval and circulated naturally. As such, this will clean the damaged area, while at the same time allowing the healing energy to seal the holes.

This form of healing is commonly referred to as "Reiki." Reiki is not a gag, it is utilizing an understanding of how the body heals on an energetic level in order to facilitate the healing of others.

True healers all around the world have used the cosmic energy, now commonly known as Reiki energy, to heal people. This is best performed by placing one's hands on the affected area and then sitting in meditation for a long period of time, in order to channel the energy appropriately. The understanding of Reiki energy has been around for a very long time across many cultures. According to my teacher, and many others, the original creator of modern "Reiki," Mikao Usui, actually learned his methods while studying in a Buddhist monastery. Most of the audience that are familiar with Mo Pai are not aware of the healing process on an energetic level because they are only focused on the martial aspects of energy cultivation.

When one relaxes, the subtle form of energy known as the cosmic energy, flows from the top of the head into the body and the arms. By placing the hands on an injured area, one is making use of this cosmic energy that is flowing into the hands. With continual meditation practice and through relaxation, one can actually become aware of the cosmic energy and learn to empower its flow.

The jing leaking out of the dantien also has some strange phenomenon associated with it. The jing is no longer inside of the dantien and it actually creates air in the stomach when leaking out. Jing represented on the physical plane is a form of air. John Chang says that the chi is in the air, but the chi is also the air itself. Similarly, many martial artists will say that chi is just air. While many of them have no idea about internal cultivation, they are actually somewhat correct. As the chi doubles as air on the physical plane it therefor creates air inside of the physical stomach when leaking out of the LDT. This leads to bloating in the lower stomach and the continual passing of gas when the energy leaves the stomach.

Besides the actual energetic and physical damage, the psychological effect from this injury can be overwhelming. The leaking sensation of vitality is something that is difficult to become accustomed to. It is ironic how in the search for Mo Pai power one can lose all of their power.

Rasputin

Grigori Rasputin was a notable healer from the late 1800's and was a prime example of the power of the cosmic energy known as Reiki.

Rasputin would enter into deep states of meditation and channel the cosmic energy through his body and into his patients. The way he would do this was by sitting behind the sick person's bed with his hands on their shoulders and remain in meditation all night while they slept. His healings were powerful because he was able to enter into absolute meditation. Most Reiki healers cannot hold concentration and are quickly lost in thought, making the channeling less powerful.

Because of Rasputin's continual successes he

eventually attracted the attention of some of the wealthiest and most influential people in Russia. And when he healed the Russian Tsarina's (Supreme Ruler) boy from hemophilia his life changed dramatically. He instantly gained a position with the royal family. Many people were angered that Rasputin, once a mere peasant, was actually living with the empress, and they were also a bit suspicious of him wooing her.[4]

Hemophilia - A.k.a. the "Royal Disease." A disorder in the blood that causes one to bleed without stopping.

Besides his powerful healings, Rasputin was also noted for his resistance to death. At one point he was actually stabbed in the stomach when returning home, after which he then had to beat his assassin off with a stick in order to drive them away. Later, after recovering, some also report that his food was poisoned multiple times, but to no avail. However, it was later noted in his autopsy that no poison was found in his system and that the poison itself was fake. Next, he was shot in the back and left on the ground assumed to be dead. But then he got back up, and tried to run away from his assailant, but then he was shot two more times. After that he was further beaten with clubs, just to be sure. Then, he was finally wrapped in a rug and thrown into the river. After this point, however, when inspecting his dead body, there were actually signs (scratch marks) of him trying to escape.[5]

Why did Rasputin have such a powerful resistance to death? The answer is most likely *yin chi*. Having attained absolute concentration, he was able to achieve levels of yin chi beyond that of the average human, providing him with a powerful layer of resistance. Similarly, John Chang also uses his yin chi in order to stop pellet gun bullets in his hand.

Many unable to rationally grasp the possibilities surrounding Rasputin's history have simply come to think that he was nothing more than an over-inflated figurehead resulting from shifting political circumstances in Russia at the time. However, when looking at his past, everything "extraordinary" that he achieved was not unique, and actually aligned with the experiences of other masters around the world. It is important to remember that Rasputin began his journey as nothing more than a simple peasant, but he was sought after, and what he had attained is that which allowed him to rise into royalty, even creating jealously among the nobility. The escalation of his status was very uncommon, an occurrence akin to "changing his stars." However, that which made him extraordinary, is that which eventually put a target on his head and lead to his brutal death. When looking at John Chang, he is also very extraordinary, it is difficult to blame him for wanting to remain nothing more than a closed door.

The Golden Aura

Periodically throughout the texts, John Chang mentions a yellow aura surrounding particular individuals. He continues to explain how it is those who are in balance with nature that attain this yellow aura.[7] The yellow aura, which is a sign of balance and harmony, is seen as superior to the white or black auras that surround those who are good and those who are evil.

The yellow aura is more commonly referred to as "the golden aura." From an alchemical standpoint, the golden aura is significant because it is often portrayed as the signature of one who has completed alchemy and become an awakened being. The true alchemist is not concerned with creating physical gold, but in actually becoming golden themselves. It is for this reason that images of Jesus, Buddha, Krishna, and various other historical enlightened beings are often depicted with having a golden aura.

John Chang recognizes the importance of those who have attained the golden aura and see it as akin to having natural talent, making it the mark of a good student. Personally, I believe these individuals make strong students because they have the ability to heal injuries and also have increased levels of concentration. It stands to reason that John's teacher, Liao Che Tung, already had the golden aura before he began training Mo Pai Nei Kung, and this gave him the ability to complete all four levels in less than one year.

It is important to note that John Chang does not directly attribute the attainment of the golden aura to his own training system or the energy centers. He instead focuses on the importance of creating balance with nature and one's surroundings. From this, one can come to the conclusion that it is important for one to be continually seeking balance in one's external life while training. Implying that an important factor of transcending the human condition is actually facing it. From a give and take perspective, to achieve balance often requires taking some form of responsibility. Overall, this concept of sustaining balance is comparable to the "Middle Way" teachings taught by Buddha.

Levitation

While reading about masters in the cultivation arts, one often comes across stories of levitation, walking on water, and even flight. Many yogis and masters have cultivated this ability in the past, and one of the most famous instances is in the Bible (Mark 6:48) where Jesus is described walking on the surface of water to reach his disciples in the boat.

When it comes to levitation both Jim McMillan and Kosta Danaos have different claims as to John Chang's ability. In one instance, Kosta Danaos describes John Chang levitating completely off of the ground. While in the other, Jim McMillan describes John Chang standing on a scale and being only capable of dramatically reducing his weight.

One can argue that this split opinion by the two students regarding John Chang's ability to levitate does not actually obstruct the possibility that he can levitate or not. In the instance with Kosta Danaos, John Chang goes into full meditation and enters into the breathless state before levitating.[7] While in the other instance, where John Chang achieves 80% weight reduction, he is standing upright on a scale and is most likely not in the breathless state.[8] These descriptions can be the difference between performing levitation in an absolute concentration state vs. normal state.

John Chang describes yin chi as being like gravity.[9] This comes as no surprise, because he is in agreeance with many other masters who say that the secret to levitation and gravity manipulation lies in the power of yin chi. Gravity has to do with the magnetic attractive force of the Earth. The ability to control gravity's effect on the body and nullify one's weight, has to do with gathering yin chi. When a master has attained an amount of yin chi in his body that corresponds to his body weight, or the gravitational force of the Earth, they will gain the ability nullify gravity and become weightless. A master who is using yin chi in this manner will hardly be in contact with the ground and can even become able to walk on water.[10]

There seems to be no limit to the amount of yin chi a master can gather. Some masters have even been described as mastering the ability of flight.[11]

Epilogue

The ancient art of Mo Pai is dual in nature. Mo Pai serves both as a destructive technology intended for war, and also as a tool for attaining conscious immortality after the death of the physical body. In truth, because of the dual nature of Mo Pai, there exist more direct paths to conscious immortality and nirvana. A large portion of the Mo Pai technology is directed towards obtaining enough life-force to handle situations that call for war and self-defense.

Mo Pai is truly a fascinating technology. A manipulation of subtle energies in such a way that can produce extraordinary capacities. However, one must not overlook the fact that many students have consistently trained in the Mo Pai practices for entire decades without transcendental achievement, even under John Chang's direct guidance. For some, Mo Pai has been an obstacle not only because of the duration, but also because of the danger that is presented.

If the "Great Work" has not been completed, one should be making every effort possible to merge with the higher conscious awareness of who one is, and why they are here. One should do what is most important first and focus entirely on achieving balance with nature, mastering the senses, and experientially merging with the primordial self. For those interested, the next book will be entirely dedicated towards understanding the process of metamorphosis and that of attaining the heavenly experience. Conscious expansion towards an enlightened understanding of reality is the greatest endeavor of man, may we all make a worthy effort.

In Remembrance,

Jim McMillan was a unique individual who had the determination and will power to step out of his comfortable everyday life and risk his general well-being in order to discover the secrets of energy cultivation. Going far out of his way to venture to the other side of the world, Jim McMillan invested both his time and energy into helping the human race reach new potentials of understanding regarding energy cultivation. Today, John Chang remains the single greatest catalyst for westerners discovering the hidden realm of energy cultivation. As the first western student, Jim McMillan played a major role both personally pursuing information from John Chang and also unlocking invaluable secrets through his own training and dedication. Equally important, Jim McMillan made himself available to serve as a teacher and sacrifice his valuable time towards helping the multiplicity of new students that came to him seeking answers.

The past, present, and future state of the western world owes a thank you to Jim McMillan's evolutionary efforts.

Notes

Introduction

1. McMillan, J. (2011). Seeking the Master of Mo Pai: Adventures with John Chang. Kentucky: Sailing Leaf Publishing.
2. Awareness, memory, and ability to create/expression.
3. The authentic levels go 1, 2a, 2b, and 3. However, for western students the levels have been simplified to level 1, 2, 3, and 4.
4. Unpublished Interview-Chi and It's Healing Energy – Time Monk Radio Network, 7/30/2011
5. (McMillan, 2011), Sailing Leaf Publishing. Reprinted with permission of publisher. Page. 37
6. A master at this stage has transcended and mastered the human body. This allows them enter the breathless state at will, causing the heartbeat to cease.
7. Unpublished Interview-Chi and It's Healing Energy – Time Monk Radio Network, 7/30/2011, Time: 20:20
8. (McMillan, 2011), Sailing Leaf Publishing. Page 72

9. (Bardon, 2013), Page 37

10. There exist many variations of spelling for this word. I prefer Dantien, instead of Dantein or Dan Tien.

11. Kosta Danaos also mentions this point on page 50 in The Magus of Java. However, for simplification purposes, and to stay consistent with the previous texts, during the training I will refer to Jing as Chi.

12. Cleary, T. (2009). Vitality, Energy, Spirit: A Taoist Sourcebook. Boston: Shambhala.

13. Some Daoist lineages would say Wuji is cultivated at this point.

14. (McMillan, 2011), Sailing Leaf Publishing. Reprinted with permission of publisher. Page. 73

Level One
SUMMONING THE FIRE

1. Chen Kaiguo, Z. S. (1998). *Opening the Dragon Gate: The Making of a Modern Taoist Wizard.* (T. Cleary Trans.) North Clarendon: Tuttle Publishing.

2. More information on the different postures effects on the energy body are also explained in Kriya Yoga.

3. Duff, L. T. (2009, June 10th). Gampopa's Mahamudra The Five Part Mahamudra of the Kagyus. ew*Padma Karpo Translation Committee* . Kathmandu , Nepal., Page. 36

4. (Bardon, 2013)

5. Walewski, C. S. (2006). *A System of Caucasian Yoga* . Whitefish: Kessinger Pub Co.

6. The color red has to do with the warm colors associated with the lower three major energy centers.

7. (McMillan, 2011), Sailing Leaf Publishing.

8. Unpublished Interview-Chi and It's Healing Energy – Time Monk Radio Network, 7/30/2011, 19:10

9. Danaos, K. (2000). *The Magus of Java: Teachings of an Authentic Taoist Immortal.* Rochester, Vermont, United States of America: Inner Traditions. Page. 82, Page 64

10. (McMillan, 2011), Sailing Leaf Publishing. Page. 40 / McMillan's training times sourced his Level 1 instructions.

11. (McMillan, 2011), Sailing Leaf Publishing. Page. 39

12. (McMillan, 2011), Sailing Leaf Publishing. Page. 221

Level Two
FORMING THE MASS

*Information regarding the level two technique was gained through multiple sources and direct accounts of Mo Pai students. This includes direct students of Jim McMillan, Kosta Danaos, and the Indonesian Mo Pai. This information is required for the direct purpose of facilitating a comprehensive understanding of more advanced aspects of the Mo Pai system.

1. (McMillan, 2011), Sailing Leaf Publishing. Page.215

2. Link: http://www.baguaquanlessons.com/crotch-3516821185.html (key aspects: 6:20 minutes).

3. The Magus of Java By Kosta Danaos published by Inner Traditions International and Bear & Company,

2000. All rights reserved.
http://www.Innertraditions.com Reprinted with permission of publisher. Page. 105

4.   (Danaos, 2000), Page. 81

5.   (McMillan, 2011), Sailing Leaf Publishing. Page. 77

6.   (McMillan, 2011), Sailing Leaf Publishing. Reprinted with permission of publisher. Page. 213

7.   (Danaos, 2000), Reprint. Page. 105

8.   (Danaos, 2000), Reprint. Page. 105

9.   (Danaos, 2000), Reprint. Page. 82

10.   (McMillan, 2011), Sailing Leaf Publishing. Reprinted with permission of publisher. Page. 182

11.   Unpublished Interview-Chi and It's Healing Energy – Time Monk Radio Network, 7/30/2011

12.   (Danaos, 2000), Reprint. Noted from observing data presented on page. 81-82.

13.   (McMillan, 2011), Sailing Leaf Publishing.

14.   (Walewski, 2006), Page. 97

15.   Holder, R. (2005). The "AntiChrist" Training Manual . San Diego , California, United States: The Sorcerer King., Page. 15

16.   The seated level 2 training is also hinted at in the Magus of Java on page 147

Level Three
HANDLING THE POWER

1.   (McMillan, 2011), Sailing Leaf Publishing. Reprinted

with permission of publisher. Page. 39

2. Unpublished Interview-Chi and It's Healing Energy – Time Monk Radio Network, 7/30/2011, Time: 25:50

3. (Danaos, 2000), Page.106

4. (Danaos, 2000), Reprint. Page. 106

5. (McMillan, 2011), Sailing Leaf Publishing. Reprinted with permission of publisher. Page.39

6. (Danaos, 2000), Reprint. Page. 106

7. (McMillan, 2011), Sailing Leaf Publishing. Reprinted with permission of publisher. Page.220

8. (McMillan, 2011), pg. 213

9. (McMillan, 2011), Sailing Leaf Publishing. Page.213

10. (McMillan, 2011), Sailing Leaf Publishing. Reprinted with permission of publisher. Page.213

11. (Danaos, 2000), Reprint. Page. 106

12. (McMillan, 2011), Sailing Leaf Publishing. pg. 212

13. (McMillan, 2011), Sailing Leaf Publishing. Page.212

14. Unpublished Interview-Chi and It's Healing Energy – Time Monk Radio Network, 7/30/2011, Time: 15:30

15. (McMillan, 2011), pg. 245

Level Four
THE IMMORTAL SPARK

1. 100 Character Tablet, Line 12, Translation by Amilia Chen.

2. (Danaos, 2000), Page. 109

3. (Danaos, 2000), Page 104

4. (Danaos, 2000), Reprint. Page. 108

5. (Danaos, 2000), Reprint. Page. 108

6. (Danaos, 2000), Reprint. 109

7. (Danaos, 2000), Reprint. 82

8. (Danaos, 2000), Reprint. Page. 97

9. (Danaos, 2000), Reprint. Page. 109

10. (Danaos, 2000), Reprint. Page. 109

11. (Danaos, 2000), pg. 97, 108

12. (McMillan, 2011), Sailing Leaf Publishing. Page. 179

13. (Danaos, 2000). Page. 97

14. (Danaos, 2000) Reprint. Page. 109

15. (McMillan, 2011), Sailing Leaf Publishing. Reprinted with permission of publisher. Page. 73

16. (McMillan, 2011) Sailing Leaf Publishing. Reprinted with permission of publisher. Page. 77

17. (Danaos, 2000), Reprint. Page. 97

18. (McMillan, 2011), Sailing Leaf Publishing. Reprint. Page. 50

19. Markides, K. C. (1989). The Magus of Strovolos: The Extraordinary World of a Spiritual Healer. London: Penguin Books. Page. 60

20. (McMillan, 2011), Sailing Leaf Publishing. Reprint. Page. 150

21. (Danaos, 2000), Reprint. Page. 97

22. (Markides, 1989), Reprint. Page. 56

23. (Chen Kaiguo, 1998), Reprint. Page. 14

24. (McMillan, 2011), Reprint. Page. 151

25. *Chakras*. (2006,220). Retrieved from Namaste: http://www.namaste.it/kundalini/kundalini_eng/chakr

as1.html

26. (McMillan, 2011), Sailing Leaf Publishing. Reprinted with permission of publisher. Page. 210

27. (McMillan, 2011), Sailing Leaf Publishing. Page. 210

28. *The Magus of Java* by Kosta Danaos published by Inner Traditions International and Bear & Company, 2000. All rights reserved. http://www.Innertraditions.com Reprinted with permission of publisher. Page. 184

29. (Danaos, 2000), Page.13

30. (Danaos, 2000), pg. 67, 89

31. The 6th vehicle, which some refer to as the greatest, is to directly observe the mind itself.

32. YouTube. (2010, October 29). Altered State – The Iceman – Wim Hof [Video file]. Retrieved from https://www.youtube.com/watch?v=sKT1Wvz3xm0 Wim also explains in Daredevils, The Iceman, 28:00 minutes, that he has awakened potentials in his spine.

Post Fusion
LEVELS 5-72

1. (McMillan, 2011), Sailing Leaf Publishing. Reprinted with permission of publisher. Page. 50

2. (Danaos, 2000), Reprint. Page 107

3. (McMillan, 2011), Sailing Leaf Publishing. Reprinted with permission of publisher. Page. 46

4. (McMillan, 2011), Sailing Leaf Publishing. Page. 86

5. (Danaos, 2000), Page. 107

6. (The Litany of Bodhidharma Bodhisattva), Page. 3

7. Bodhidharma. (2015). Retrieved from International Budo Institute: http://www.i-budo.com/library/zen-masters/bodhidharma/

8. (Danaos, 2000), Page. 73

9. (Danaos, 2000), Page. 74

10. (McMillan, 2011), Sailing Leaf Publishing. Reprinted with permission of the publisher. Page. 154, 155

11. http://thetaobums.com/topic/21718-released-seeking-the-master-of-mo-pai-adventures-with-john-chang-by-jim-mcmillan/page-10

12. (Chen Kaiguo, 1998), Page. 210

13. (Chen Kaiguo, 1998), Reprinted with permission of publisher. Page. 22

14. (Chen Kaiguo, 1998), Page. 62

15. Lao Zi Academy. (n.d.). Retrieved from http://www.laoziacademy.us/Wang%20Liping%20story.htm

16. Sell, W. (2015). *The Secret of the Golder Flower*.Retrieved from http://thesecretofthegoldenflower.com

17. (Danaos, 2000), Page. 89

18. Assuming 80 hours, Kostas Danaos teaches 81 hours.

19. (Danaos, 2000), Reprint. Page. 74

20. (Danaos, 2000), Page. 64

21. (Danaos, 2000), Reprint. Page. 67

22. (Danaos, 2000), Page. 107

23. Y=160x-480, assuming 80 hours

24. (Danaos, 2000), Page. 129

25. (Chen Kaiguo, 1998), Page. 50

26. (Danaos, 2000), 98
27. Flaws, B. (1991). The Tao of Healthy Eating: Dietary Wisdom According to Traditional Chinese Medicine. Boulder: Blue Poppy Press.
28. (Chen Kaiguo, 1998)
29. (Danaos, 2000), pg. 98
30. Ping, W. L. (29 March 2012). Ling Bao Tong Zhi Neng Nei Gong Shu. (R. Liao, Trans.) Printed by CreateSpace.
31. (Danaos, 2000), Page. 40
32. (Chen Kaiguo, 1998), Page. 50
33. (Markides, 1989), Page. 121
34. (Danaos, 2000), Reprint. Page. 38
35. (Danaos, 2000), Page. 88
36. (McMillan, 2011), Sailing Leaf Publishing. Page. 37
37. (Chen Kaiguo, 1998)
38. (Danaos, 2000), Page. 67
39. (Markides, 1989)

Going Further

1. (Danaos, 2000), Page. 105
2. (McMillan, 2011), Reprint. Page.73
3. Information received from discussions on www.TheTaoBums.com
4. (Rosenberg, 2000)
5. (Rosenberg, 2000)
6. (Citation Removed)
7. (Danaos, 2000)
8. (Danaos, 2000), Page. 158

9. (McMillan, 2011), Sailing Leaf Publishing. Page. 146

10. (Danaos, 2000), Page. 204

11. (Bardon, 2013), Page. 349

12. See Alexandra David Neel - Magic and Magicians in Tibet.

Bibliography

Bardon, F. (2013). *Initiation into Hermetics.* Holladay: Merkur Pub Company.

Billy, S. (2010, October 29). Altered State - The Iceman - Wim Hof. [Video file], Retrieved from https://www.youtube.com/watch?v=sKT1Wvz3xm0.

Bodhidharma. (2015). Retrieved from International Budo Institute: http://www.i-budo.com/library/zen-masters/bodhidharma/

Chakras. (2006, 2 20). Retrieved from Namaste: http://www.namaste.it/kundalini/kundalini_eng/chakras1.html

Chen Kaiguo, Z. S. (1998). *Opening the Dragon Gate: The Making of a Modern Taoist Wizard.* (T. Cleary, Trans.) North Clarendon: Tuttle Publishing.

Cleary, T. (2009). *Vitality, Energy, Spirit: A Taoist Sourcebook.* Boston: Shambhala.

Danaos, K. (2000). *The Magus of Java: Teachings of an Authentic Taoist Immortal.* Rochester, Vermont , United States of America: Inner Traditions.

David-Neel, M. A. (1971). *Magic and Mystery in Tibet.* Mineola, New York: Dover Publications.

Duff, L. T. (2009, June 10th). Gampopa's Mahamudra The Five Part Mahamudra of the Kagyus. *Padma Karpo Translation Committee* . Kathmandu , Nepal.

Flaws, B. (1991). *The Tao of Healthy Eating: Dietary Wisdom According to Traditional Chinese Medicine.* Boulder: Blue Poppy Press.

Holder, R. (2005). The "AntiChrist" Training Manual . San Diego , California, United States: The Sorcerer King.

Lao Zi Academy. (n.d.). Retrieved from http://www.laoziacademy.us/Wang%20Liping%20story.htm

Markides, K. C. (1989). *The Magus of Strovolos: The Extraordinary World of a Spiritual Healer.* London: Penguin Books.

McMillan, J. (2011). *Seeking the Master of Mo Pai: Adventures with John Chang.* Kentucky: Sailing Leaf Publishing.

Ping, W. L. (29 March 2012). *Ling Bao Tong Zhi Neng Nei Gong Shu.* (R. Liao, Trans.) Printed by CreateSpace.

Sell, W. (2015). *The Secret of the Golder Flower.* Retrieved from http://thesecretofthegoldenflower.com/

The Litany of Bodhidharma Bodhisattva. (n.d.). *Shasta Abbey.* Mt. Shasta, California.

Walewski, C. S. (2006). *A System of Caucasian Yoga* . Whitefish: Kessinger Pub Co.

Recommended Reading

Seeking the Master of Mo Pai: Adventures with John Chang – Jim McMillan

    Seeking the Master of Mo Pai conveys the remarkable story of Jim McMillan's adventure uncovering the secrets behind the ancient esoteric art of Mo Pai. Jim McMillan describes in detail his wonderful and extraordinary experiences with the legendary master John Chang. Throughout the text Jim McMillan also shares his profound knowledge that he accumulated from personally studying the esoteric world from multiple sects and lineages outside of the Mo Pai. He gives his insight into these various schools and practices and also compares them with the Mo Pai training that he learned directly from John Chang. Being a dedicated practitioner of the Mo Pai, Jim McMillan also describes in detail the sensations and personal experiences that he felt and witnessed throughout his dedicated training. Anyone with serious interest in the Mo Pai training will invest their time into studying this text.

The Magus of Java: Teachings of an Authentic Taoist Immortal – Kosta Danaos

    The Magus of Java shares Kosta Danaos's adventures and experiences with the Mo Pai lineage. In this book Danaos describes in detail his dialog with the legendary master John

Chang. As such, this book provides a large amount of information regarding the Mo Pai lineage and its practices. Danaos does an excellent job finding answers regarding many of the profound questions regarding the Mo Pai training and its history. The book is written in a way that can attract anyone from any background regardless of their level of seriousness towards energy cultivation practices. That being said, anyone with interest in Mo Pai will also invest their time into reading this text.

Additional Reading:

Enter the Dragon Gate: The Making of a Modern Taoist Wizard – Chen Kaigou/Zheng Shunchao

Initiation into Hermetics – Franz Bardon

The Magus of Strovolos: The Extraordinary World of a Spiritual Healer – Kyriacos C. Markides

www.JamesVanGelder.com

Made in the USA
San Bernardino, CA
13 July 2017